Contemplation

NO LIMITS

NO LIMITS

Edited by Costica Bradatan

The most important questions in life haunt us with a sense of boundlessness: there is no one right way to think about them or an exclusive place to look for answers. Philosophers and prophets, poets and scholars, scientists and artists—all are right in their quest for clarity and meaning. We care about these issues not simply in themselves but for ourselves—for us. To make sense of them is to understand who we are better. No Limits brings together creative thinkers who delight in the pleasure of intellectual hunting, wherever the hunt may take them and whatever critical boundaries they have to trample as they go. And in so doing they prove that such searching is not just rewarding but also transformative. There are no limits to knowledge and self-knowledge—just as there are none to self-fashioning.

Aimlessness, Tom Lutz
Intervolution: Smart Bodies Smart Things, Mark C. Taylor
Touch: Recovering Our Most Vital Sense, Richard Kearney
Inwardness: An Outsider's Guide, Jonardon Ganeri
Self-Improvement: Technologies of the Soul in the Age of Artificial Intelligence, Mark Coeckelbergh
Taste: A Book of Small Bites, Jehanne Dubrow
Storythinking: The New Science of Narrative Intelligence, Angus Fletcher
Rapture, Christopher Hamilton

Contemplation

Kevin Hart

THE MOVEMENTS
OF THE SOUL

Columbia University Press
New York

Columbia University Press
Publishers Since 1893
New York   Chichester, West Sussex
cup.columbia.edu
Copyright © 2024 Columbia University Press
All rights reserved

Library of Congress Cataloging-in-Publication Data
Title: Contemplation : the movements of the soul / Kevin Hart.
Description: New York : Columbia University Press, [2024] |
    Series: No limits | Includes bibliographical references and index.
Identifiers: LCCN 2023050335 (print) |
    LCCN 2023050336 (ebook) |
    ISBN 9780231213462 (hardback) |
    ISBN 9780231213479 (trade paperback) |
    ISBN 9780231559904 (ebook)
Subjects: LCSH: Contemplation—Comparative studies. |
    Christianity and other religions. | Contemplation—Philosophy.
Classification: LCC BV5091.C7 .H377 2024 (print) |
    LCC BV5091.C7 (ebook) | DDC 248.3/4—dc23/eng/20240319
LC record available at https://lccn.loc.gov/2023050335
LC ebook record available at https://lccn.loc.gov/2023050336

Printed and bound by CPI Group (UK) Ltd, Croydon, CR0 4YY

Cover design: Chang Jae Lee

for Jack

> I haste
> To contemplate undazzled some one truth,
> Its bearings and effects alone—at once
> What was a speck expands into a star,
> Asking a life to pass exploring thus.
>
> —ROBERT BROWNING, *Paracelsus*

Contents

Acknowledgments *xi*

Introduction 1
1. First Thoughts About Contemplation 3
2. Questions of Practice and Cognition 31
3. Ways of Contemplating 59
4. What to Contemplate 89
5. Why Contemplate? 115

Notes *135*

Further Reading *143*

Index *145*

Acknowledgments

I am thankful to Gavin Flood and John Nemec, who checked my remarks on Buddhism and Hinduism; to Ahmed al-Rahim, who helped me clarify my thoughts on Islam; and to Greg Goering, who did the same with regard to Judaism. Philip Gates and Walter Jost read the whole book in draft and, as always, were great encouragements. My wife, Sashanna Hart, read a fair draft of the whole and improved each chapter by her suggestions, for which I am very grateful. I am grateful to the two anonymous readers of the typescript, each of whom made useful recommendations. Finally, I thank the editorial and production staff at Columbia University Press for their splendid work in bringing the book into the world.

Introduction

This is a book on contemplation. It is not a guide that tells you how to contemplate God, although Christians in particular will find here several esteemed ways of doing just that. Nor is it a survey of different practice of contemplation in world religions, although some remarks on Buddhist, Christian, Hindu, and Pagan practices are offered. Nor does it propose a thoroughgoing philosophy or theology of contemplation, let alone contribute to mystical theology; however, several philosophers, theologians and mystics are discussed, in order to clarify questions and extend the conversation as it goes along. Nor is it an introduction to the emerging field of contemplative studies. Little or nothing is said about education, psychology, or neuroscience, or artistic or clinical uses of contemplation.

Rather, this book initiates readers into the general study of the movements of the soul, understood both in a sacred and a secular manner: how we reflect upon our moral and mortal selves, learn discursively about invisible phenomena and their truths, and transcend the world or even

INTRODUCTION

ourselves. It examines a range of religious, aesthetic, and philosophical notions of contemplation while remaining chiefly focused on retrieving sources from Catholic and (to some extent) Orthodox Christianity. First of all, we need to distinguish several senses of the word "contemplation" and to set aside some possible confusions. Then we must pass to questions of practice and the different modes of cognition that are involved when exercising the soul. Two or three traditional ways of beholding God are presented, and then the horizon widens so that we can consider whether or not anything can be contemplated other than the deity. Finally, we ask ourselves, "Why contemplate?" Some objections to the practice are entertained, and some reasons why it should be pursued are proposed.

1
First Thoughts About Contemplation

What is contemplation? The question is a good deal simpler than any answer that can be offered. Some contemporary responses will begin by identifying the cultural and religious heritages of one or another form of contemplation, usually drawing from Asian wisdom. We shall often be told that contemplation is practiced mostly in Buddhism, Daoism, and Hinduism, and these days it is widely assumed that it occurs only in those and other Asian religions. Yet, if we consider the word over its fullest semantic range, we shall also find versions of contemplation in Islam and Judaism. Perhaps most surprisingly for many secular people in the West, Christianity has a deep and rich tradition of beholding God, much of which is overlooked or misunderstood, not only in Protestantism but also in Catholicism after Vatican II (1962–1965). Much of what I have to say in this little book will turn on recovering elements of the Catholic and Orthodox heritages of contemplation.[1] Even so, as those adept in Christian

FIRST THOUGHTS ABOUT CONTEMPLATION

spirituality will readily testify, there is much to be learned from Asian wisdom in this regard.

No sooner has the assumption that contemplation derives solely from Asian religions been identified and questioned than another assumption presents itself. Is it inherently religious? In pondering the question, we inevitably reflect that Buddhism and Christianity, for example, disclose very different profiles of "religion." Christianity is strictly a theistic religion: it is oriented to the worship of God, who is believed to have created and redeemed the world. Buddhism, however, is not a theistic religion but, rather, a quest for spiritual enlightenment in oneself and others. Siddhartha Gautama, later known as the Buddha, was from the Gangetic plains of the Indian subcontinent (now part of Nepal). His death is traditionally dated to 400 BC. He was of royal family, yet, despite enjoying a life of plenty, he awoke from a state of ignorance about reality and then wandered in India, teaching others. He is not praised as God or a god by his followers, but is for them a revered model of moderate asceticism and moral discipline known as the "middle way." Nonetheless, some non-Western Buddhists believe that there are non-gods, anti-gods, ghosts, and hell beings, who can help or hinder one on the way to enlightenment, and the Mahāyāna traditions have Buddhas as virtual gods. (In Pure Land Buddhism, Amitābha functions as a god.) By contrast, in Christianity, one seeks, through the aid of the Holy Spirit, to become more and more like Christ, who is himself the image of the Father. Interference comes from sin and its effects, to be sure, but it can be overcome through what Western Christians call "grace." Christian contemplation, then, is

FIRST THOUGHTS ABOUT CONTEMPLATION

undertaken, at least in its higher reaches, as a means of attaining union with the deity.

Not so in Buddhism: there contemplation is pursued in order to free one from anger, anxiety, fear, jealousy, and other defilements, as well as to detach one from the persistent thorns of troublesome longings; it is an effort of concentrating the body, mind, and heart so that one might come to collect oneself and understand the world without illusion. In gaining wisdom, one quenches unwholesome desires of the earthly mind and, if one persists with the discipline, achieves release from greed, aversion, and ignorance in this life (as well as escaping from the cycle of death and rebirth). In the language of the religion, one attains nirvana, which for most Buddhists is not a place ("the further shore") but a state of being: a final delivery from suffering. From the very beginning of one's training in *bhāvanā* (mental development), emphasis is placed on how one positions the body and in how one regulates one's breath. Overly sharp distinctions between mind and body dissolve, for each is disclosed to be involved in the other. Christian teachers of contemplative prayer will also point beginners to the need to sit upright in a particular space—quiet, partly dark, free from distraction and interruption—and to synchronize one's breathing with one's heartbeat so that one may begin to attune oneself to God.

General parallels between Eastern and Western practices are well worth noticing, as are their many divergences. Equally, one needs to acknowledge that there are many distinct spiritual exercises in each of Buddhism and Christianity, along with the other religions we have been considering. How a Tibetan Buddhist nun addresses herself to her spiritual discipline will differ in some ways (and at some stages) from how a Zen Buddhist sits in a meditation hall before a master in Tokyo or San Francisco, and both will differ from how a Pure Land Buddhist in Japan cultivates his or her spiritual development. Where the Tibetan, in the first of the five rituals, may be seen whirling clockwise in order to enhance her physical and mental health, those engaging in Zen will sit in conversation with a teacher. They will ponder koans, riddles strongly peppered with paradox to stimulate doubt in the comprehensive power of the analytic mind so as to break through rigid mental categories. Meanwhile, the Pure Land Buddhist will conduct exercises of visualization, often beginning with trying to imagine the setting sun as precisely as possible, in order to focus consciousness. Diverse practices ultimately lead, however, to roughly the same end: clarity and quietness of mind, a higher degree of compassion and receptiveness to other people, and an ability to regard everything in fresh terms. Similarly, in Christianity, how a Dominican friar engages in mental prayer is not exactly the same as how an Orthodox monk committed to hesychasm pursues his daily life. The one will spend periods of time in silent mental prayer, as well as in choir and study, while the other will repeat the Jesus Prayer endlessly, regardless of what else he is doing.[2] Both aim to simplify their hearts and minds so as to become more and more like the God they worship, whose being is held to be utterly simple: love itself.

Not all contemplation is religious in the ways I have just evoked. Some contemplative practices are neither modes of prayer to the deity nor disciplines of detachment from desire with the aim of freeing oneself from temporal cares.

FIRST THOUGHTS ABOUT CONTEMPLATION

We might be tempted to say that some contemplation is philosophical, not religious, but, in doing so, we must be very careful not to suggest that either Buddhist or Christian usage (to restrict ourselves to just those two) has no philosophical dimension. Both activities are concerned with making a shift in how we know things (epistemology); both have ideas about the nature of reality and truth (metaphysics); both reflect on how we think (logic); both are deeply concerned with how one should act (ethics); and both have views about what philosophy should and should not do (metaphilosophy). To be sure, there are contemplative pursuits that at first seem more overtly philosophical than religious: the spiritual exercises of the ancient Greeks, for example, which we shall consider later in this book. Closer examination of these Epicurean, Stoic, and Platonic exercises generate second thoughts, though, about whether there can be a firm, unbroken, straight line between philosophy and religion as we understand them today. The old spiritual exercises may not have been widely practiced by the votaries of Greek cultic religion, but they were nonetheless of intense significance, for they helped contemporaries of a thoughtful cast of mind to come to terms with suffering and mortality and to enhance their experiences of life.

The venerable couple of religion and philosophy does not exhaust all that can be said about our theme, however. For practices that were once firmly embedded in religious contexts—Buddhist, Christian, Daoist, Hindu, Jewish, or Islamic—can readily be secularized, and this process does not thereby make them more overtly philosophical, in the modern, Western sense of an academic discipline. Indeed, it might well occlude their philosophical character as fully

FIRST THOUGHTS ABOUT CONTEMPLATION

as it does their religious character. This is the case with mindfulness, with its deep roots in Buddhism, in which it is known as *smṛti* (Sanskrit, "memory," or "awareness"; *sati* in Pali) and is now widely adapted for secular use in the West. This technique of attending to one's breath is commended in the Western medical world for help in overcoming anxiety, lowering blood pressure, treating heart disease, and, in general, alleviating the fretting and fussing of modern life. The hive of the mind is stilled. Many of the advocates of mindfulness, especially in the clinical world, know of contemplation only by way of Buddhism (and usually rather distantly at best). Certainly, few in the medical community follow what Buddhists call breathing mindfulness in any detail, as, for instance, in commending the sixteen distinct stages of accomplishing it. A desire to keep the rigorously secular Western medical system free of religion, especially the Abrahamic faiths (Judaism, Christianity, and Islam) attracts them to the nontheistic nature of Buddhism, even when their patients happen to be Jewish, Christian, or Islamic. Yet these patients could learn just as well from activities that would sustain them in their chosen faith as well as improve their health.

Aware of the difficulty of tracing unwavering lines between philosophy and religion, not to mention between the secular and the religious, we might nonetheless point to certain contemplative forms that seem to owe more to philosophy than to religion. For Aristotle (384–22 BC), philosophers are the most happy of mortals because, like the gods, they can reflect on the highest things that can be known. The philosopher fulfills himself in pursuing reason and, although he may have developed few or indeed

FIRST THOUGHTS ABOUT CONTEMPLATION

many virtues, surpasses the active person who lives a virtuous life. Notice, though, that, even here, when praising the philosophical life, Aristotle invokes the gods. True, it is debated whether the reference to the gods is conventional or heartfelt, and, of course, the gods, for Aristotle, are conceived as the "first things," not as the fallible deities of Greek mythology. Theology, the study of the unmoved mover, is certainly primary, but natural science is secondary, with math coming third. One can live a contemplative life, somewhat beneath the peak that human wisdom affords, by pondering the principles of what changes or moves. So, there is natural contemplation, and to pursue it is no small achievement.

Another mode of contemplation not leagued with religion comes into view in the late eighteenth and early nineteenth centuries. There, one finds philosophers who have acclaimed aesthetic attention. One can gaze thoughtfully at a landscape, for example, and find release from one's daily troubles in the experience. One can listen to music in a quiet, still manner and reduce the chaos of one's mind. And one can read a poem slowly, opening oneself to new ways of engaging with the world and, in doing so, gain new horizons. As the Argentinian poet Roberto Juarroz (1925–1995) observes, when reading a poem contemplatively one broods on the whole language gathered behind each word.[3] Put generally, one passes from looking at things to seeing them. For some philosophers, like Edmund Husserl (1859–1938) and Ludwig Wittgenstein (1889–1951), one can even come to regard philosophy itself as a mode of contemplation, just as the Greeks did long ago, although in quite other keys. In thinking philosophically about something, one can pass from one's usual

FIRST THOUGHTS ABOUT CONTEMPLATION

habits of cognition to other ways that reveal reality more broadly or more intensely. Sometimes one can begin to see the world in all its pristine strangeness; one can look in wonder at what before was no more than an all-too-familiar scene, event, or situation. In the *Metaphysics,* Aristotle says that philosophy begins in wonder, and, in the *Nicomachean Ethics,* he observes, as we have seen, that the happy person is the one who lives the contemplative life.[4] The two things are closely related.

▶ ▷ ▶

I have already uncovered several assumptions in our everyday talk about our theme and drawn a number of distinctions in order to keep confusion at bay. But we are still far from being clear about how to use the word "contemplation" in all relevant circumstances. For one thing, I have been using it as an umbrella term for many forms and rituals that involve religion and philosophy, Western and Eastern culture, the body and the mind, and have sought to deflect overly sharp ways of distinguishing these dualities. As we shall see later, there is a place for pointed and sometimes fine distinctions when thinking about, and when performing, some modes of contemplation, but not all differences can be nicely articulated by way of smooth, uninterrupted lines. Sometimes, if one looks clearly and openly, the lines are irregular, discontinuous, or wavy. This is the case when we come to question whether we have been right thus far to speak only of contemplation. Is there not a distinction between contemplation and meditation? Even before we consider the question, we must duly acknowledge that the two words have long been often taken as synonyms.

FIRST THOUGHTS ABOUT CONTEMPLATION

One reads of Buddhist contemplation and meditation almost indifferently in many guides on the subject, and this is partly because of the difficulty of rendering Sanskrit words (or their Pali equivalents), including *smṛti*, *samādhi*, and *vipaśyanā*, into English. There is some controversy within Buddhism about the relation of *samādhi* and *vipaśyanā*, but for our purposes we may see them as complementary paths for the person seeking enlightenment, the former placing weight on mental concentration, and the latter the gaining of insight into the nature of reality. Both are needed if one is to be awoken from the thick blanket of ignorance that covers human existence. One begins with *smṛti*, concentration on one's breathing, and progresses to *samādhi*, the final stage of stillness, or, if one follows *vipassana*, one blossoms so as to see the emptiness of all things (as one hears in Mahāyāna), which is what they truly are, and in doing so gains compassion for all sentient life. In Christianity, however, there is a useful distinction between "meditation" and "contemplation," even though the two words have often been used interchangeably (as in the twelfth and seventeenth centuries), and it can be challenging to find exactly where and how it abides. One of the tasks of a spiritual director is to ascertain just where the soul who is being truly guided is on the path to God, whether in meditation, or when about to cross over into contemplation, or when actually beholding God, whether actively or passively. It is important for the director to discern the differences, for many people experience spiritual dryness, even acute distress, either in passing to contemplation or in regressing to meditation.

In general, Christian meditation involves attention to sacred images, plastic or textual, such as are gathered from

FIRST THOUGHTS ABOUT CONTEMPLATION

Scripture, and offers the soul the opportunity to digest them as thoroughly as possible and so grow in maturity. In the Middle Ages, people said that one chewed on what was offered to meditation: the process could be protracted, even after the period set for meditation was long over, and one was busy working at other tasks. To meditate on something is to get to know it more intimately, to apply it to one's own life, and to learn about how to live more closely with God. It is a search for what has been relatively unknown to the soul, and, eventually, it makes the unknown somewhat more familiar. Usually, meditation is discursive: the mind considers a situation as part of a narrative, as when performing the stations of the cross in Holy Week or, less obviously, when praying before an icon. One may project oneself into a scene, imagining oneself to be with the Virgin and the child Jesus, if one is gazing at an icon, or envisioning oneself accompanying Jesus on the path to Calvary if one is praying the stations of the cross. In doing so, one's imagination is engaged, and one erases some of the distances—emotional, cultural, and historical— between oneself and the object of meditation.

Not all meditation is confined to musing on sacred images, however. In the middle of the twelfth century, the Cistercian abbot St. Bernard of Clairvaux (1090–1153) wrote five books on an inductive form of meditation that he sent to one of his former monks, now raised to the heights of the papacy and beleaguered by many calls on his time. They were written to calm Eugenius III and to help him retain a measure of spiritual stillness in the midst of unaccustomed Church politics and intrigue. Under the sign of consideration, one is invited to reflect on oneself from several directions. First of all, one asks: Do I know myself?

FIRST THOUGHTS ABOUT CONTEMPLATION

That is, do I know my specific gifts and how well do I use them with respect to myself and others? If God has made me one sort of person, able to do some things but not others, then I cannot be another sort; I must learn how to make the most of who I am, not try to be someone else. Second, one asks: Have I acted properly toward those for whom I am responsible? Then: Have I acted well toward my peers? Then: Have I done all that I ought to do for those placed in positions above me? And finally: Have I fulfilled all my obligations to God? In considering oneself and others, one sees oneself (including one's limitations and one's faults) more sharply than otherwise; it is like looking into a mirror of obligations and adjusting how one will act over the coming day, week, or month. One begins to see the truth about oneself as a moral and spiritual being and is given an opportunity to reform.

Contemplation, however, is standardly regarded as less a search for the truth, whether about oneself or others, than as a simple intuition of God as truth. Intuition, here, is not a matter of instinct but of the intellect: there is an immediate insight into the deity or, perhaps more accurately, into a loving relationship that one enjoys with the deity. In finding God, one reposes perfectly secure in him as the truth, free from discursive thought. Meditation helps one to find God; contemplation is resting in him. Before going any further, I need to enter a caveat: I have said "standardly regarded," since there are other accounts of contemplation that are both interesting and valuable, and we shall ponder some of these as we go along, as well as probe the idea just entertained of having a simple intuition of God. Suffice it to say for now that there is agreement that there are grades of beholding, although no

FIRST THOUGHTS ABOUT CONTEMPLATION

consensus as to how many, and not everyone who practices meditation can be assured of reaching the pinnacle of mental prayer, which is union with God. Some people pass from meditation to contemplation and then fall back a step or two, either because meditation remains familiar and comforting or because they cannot sustain attention on the divine for very long. Meditation is always needed as a path to contemplation, and yet there are people for whom, once they can behold God, it seems intolerably laborious and tiresome. The ligature, as it is called, in passing from meditation to contemplation, is something spiritual directors must learn to discern, as well as offering sound advice as to how to negotiate it for the benefit of each soul.

So far it might seem that meditation and contemplation are intellectual acts. One seeks to probe sacred images in order to know them better, or one considers one's situation in life in order to know how to act more completely or effectively. And contemplation is intellectual intuition. Thus, another caution is needed. Intellectual intuition requires a movement of the will, specifically of love, in order to occur. Today, we talk of the will as the mental faculty for deliberating how and when to act. We often think of it in terms of purpose, striving, even force. In late antiquity and long after, though, it was marked more strongly than now that the will is the faculty where love abides. Love is not only an emotion (among other things) but also a willing of the good for oneself and others, the ultimate good being intimacy with God. One cannot gain insight into God as truth without first loving God and neighbor. One cannot meditate satisfactorily on sacred images without also being moved by them, by allowing them to engage one's emotions. Indeed,

FIRST THOUGHTS ABOUT CONTEMPLATION

one cannot consider the state of one's soul without being affected by the blemishes one sometimes finds there and feeling a need to do better in life.

▶ ▷ ▶

The idea that contemplation is a simple intellectual intuition of God requires us to make other discriminations in the service of finding our way through the maze in which we quickly find ourselves when thinking about our subject. The most important of these is to separate, insofar as one can, contemplation and mysticism. It is a delicate operation, one that will take some time to perform. The English word "mysticism" goes back to the Greek word μύω (transliterated *múō*), which means "I close" or "I hide." We think of an initiate's response to being shown secret rituals or told hidden truths: one must close the eyes in order not to gaze openly upon the sacred and close the lips so as not to communicate holy truths to the profane. (The Greek word for "initiate" is μύστης [transl. *mustes*].) Someone initiated into a rite enters into a relation with a mystery, whether pagan (as with the Eleusinian Mysteries) or biblical (as with the sacrament of the Eucharist). In late antiquity we find talk of "mystical theology"—discourse about the hiddenness of God from mortal eyes and ears. The Hebrew Scriptures beautifully speak time and again of God hiding himself in darkness. His holiness is so overwhelming and so intense that it cannot be directly encountered; it would kill even a righteous and beloved mortal (Exod. 33:20, RSV). When Moses is about to climb Mount Sinai, he approaches "the thick darkness where God was" (Exod. 20:21); Solomon declares that the Lord "would dwell

FIRST THOUGHTS ABOUT CONTEMPLATION

in thick darkness" (1 Kings 8:12), and the Psalmist sings, "He made darkness his covering around him" (Ps. 18:11).

Sometime in the late fifth or early sixth century, an anonymous Syrian monk wrote a very brief work called *The Mystical Theology*. He signed himself Dionysius the Areopagite, after the Greek judge whom St. Paul converted after preaching on the Areopagus in Athens (Acts 17:34). Not writing in one's own name was a common gesture of humility at the time, one that people would expect a monk to observe, but many in the following centuries took the author to be the very man converted by St. Paul, which gave his writings tremendous authority in the Middle Ages. St. Thomas Aquinas (1225–1274) quotes Dionysius over 1700 times, a number that vies with how often he quotes Aristotle (2095) or even St. Augustine (3156). The dating of the Dionysian corpus to the apostolic period was contested as early as the fifteenth and sixteenth centuries. Only in the late nineteenth century, though, did philologists feel sufficiently confident that traces of a work by the Neoplatonist philosopher Proclus (d. 485) can be found in Dionysius's writings, which is why scholars refer to him as Pseudo-Dionysius. If Proclus's *Elements of Theology* is a source for *The Mystical Theology*, Dionysius could not possibly be the man converted by St. Paul. (To maintain that *The Mystical Theology* was in fact written by the biblical Dionysius, as the Orthodox liturgy that commemorates him as hieromartyr supposes, would require finding adequate evidence of his ideas in Plato's dialogues and Aristotle's treatises, presumably some of the same passages that Proclus himself knew well.)

Pseudo-Dionysius begins *The Mystical Theology* by praying to the Trinity, asking to be guided "beyond unknowing

FIRST THOUGHTS ABOUT CONTEMPLATION

and light," to where the divine mysteries abide "simple, absolute, and unchangeable." These mysteries may be found only "in the brilliant darkness of a hidden silence"; they are "wholly unsensed and unseen." Mystical theology is the (almost impossible) exploration of this "brilliant darkness."[5] One does so by recognizing in all humility that one cannot speak properly of God, for he is above or beyond any and all human conceptions of being. Even to affirm God as good cannot be straightforwardly true, despite being scriptural, since we are in no position to understand the Trinity's ineffable goodness, which is far higher than any good that we can name, and to deny that he is good cannot be true, either, since we cannot disregard the ample testimony of scripture that he is good (e.g., Exod. 34:6; 1 Chron. 16:34; Ps. 25:8; Mark 10:18).

God has many names, all taken from the Scriptures, Pseudo-Dionysius says in another treatise, *The Divine Names*, and the Good is the highest of them. Others include Life, Light, Righteousness, Power, and Wisdom. All of these varied names refer to God as a whole, not just to one of the divine persons or to divine attributes, and all of them exceed any creaturely sense we might ascribe to them. So to call God "being" is to name something above or beyond any human understanding of being that one might entertain, while to call God "wisdom" is to name a mode of wisdom above or beyond any manner of understanding to which one might wish to point in this world. And so on. It is important not to think that because God's mode of being is completely unlike any human conception of being that he therefore does not exist, or to suppose that because his mode of wisdom is very unlike our own that he is therefore not wise. On the contrary, the

FIRST THOUGHTS ABOUT CONTEMPLATION

Pseudo-Dionysius maintains that God exists in an eminent manner, and the same goes for the eminence of the divine wisdom, the divine righteousness, the divine life, and all the others.

On a first pass, then, we might say that mystical theology attempts to speak of God as he is, above and beyond the reach of all human categories, and to reflect on how human language can be used, however inadequately, to talk about God. For the Pseudo-Dionysius, God is veiled not just in darkness, an absence of light, as the Hebrew Scriptures lyrically testify, but in conceptual darkness, an absence of appropriate mental categories. In order to draw near to him, one must plunge "into the truly mysterious darkness of unknowing."[6] The soul is not static; it moves in particular ways toward God, as we shall see. To be sure, one will never know God in the way we know items in the cosmos: he is incomprehensible. But one can approach him by gradually releasing him, as it were, from all unrevealed categories and only in and through the darkness without the slightest flicker of light to guide one. When we talk of God he is always neither X nor not-X, for he transcends both terms. But mystical theology is more than talking about God; it is also talking to God, drawing close to him in what the Greeks call ἀγάπη (transl. *agápē*), which means the unconditional love that God has for us and that we are called to have for him. To answer the call is to repent and, with grace, guard one's heart and mind so as to resist temptation and live a life pleasing to God.

This way of thinking theologically must be distinguished from the more familiar style of theology known in the Greek church as "cataphatic." The word comes from the Greek κατα (transl. *kata*), which means "down" or "into"

FIRST THOUGHTS ABOUT CONTEMPLATION

and the verb φάναι (transl. *phánai*), meaning "I speak." Cataphatic theology is the elaboration of what the Holy Spirit reveals to us in Scripture and in Christ. It is a theology of light. Yet, as already noticed, there is another way of doing theology, in which the soul moves upward into darkness, by using what has been revealed and forever drawing attention to the inadequacy of our language and concepts as a vehicle of God's word. In following this theology one passes away from any and all straightforward predications attached to the deity; even those affirmed by revelation must be deepened. It is known as apophatic theology. Once again, the adjective joins together two Greek words, the preposition ἄπό (transl. *apó*), meaning "away from," and the verb φάναι, which we have just encountered. Apophatic theology seeks to speak of God and to God by deflecting both positive and negative predicates regarding him. None will be adequate to the God beyond being.

This is not all that we need to know, even in a preliminary way, about mysticism, which merges several currents, philosophical and literary, as well as religious, from the Greeks as well as the Jews, long before modern psychology engages with it. It assumes different forms: we find apophatic mysticism, as just evoked, and we also find bridal mysticism, in which the soul is betrothed to Christ. Also one finds mysticism that is celebrated by the Church and mysticism that is condemned by it: Margaret Porette (1250–1310) was burned at the stake for her views as given in *The Mirror of Simple Souls*, and Madame Guyon (1648–1717) was imprisoned in the Bastille for her spiritual writings. In some mystical texts we hear florid personal exclamations of love—for example, Angela of Folino (1248–1309) and Richard Methley (d. 1527)—while others, such as

FIRST THOUGHTS ABOUT CONTEMPLATION

Richard of Victor (1110–1173) are strictly impersonal. We shall touch on some of these as we go on. Now, though, we need to consider mystical reading.

Centuries before the Pseudo-Dionysius wrote a word, and long before Proclus read a line of Greek philosophy, close attention was being given to what became known as the mystical reading of Scripture—the discovery of hidden meanings in the Hebrew and even the Christian writings—and this understanding of mystical reading plays into mystical theology. To understand what this mystical reading is, we must first step back to ancient Greek ways of reading Homer's epic poems the *Iliad* and the *Odyssey* in an allegorical manner. This adjective joins together two perfectly ordinary Greek words: ἄλλος (transl. *állos*), meaning "other," and ἀγορεύω (transl. *agoreúō*), meaning "I speak in the assembly." To read allegorically is to allow a text to proclaim another meaning than the one it does if one merely attends to its surface meaning.

Theagenes of Rhegium (latter half of the sixth century BC) was one of the first Greek commentators to read Homer's epic poems so as to find more profound meanings than those that constellate at their literal level. So the battle of the gods in book 20 of the *Iliad* became, for Theagenes, not a spectacle of violent behavior caused by Zeus suspending his prudent injunction for the gods not to intervene in the Trojan war but a vivid account of physical and psychological forces. What was regarded as unedifying in Homer was thoroughly redeemed by allegory. In a similar manner, though centuries later, Philo Judaeus (ca. 20 BC– ca. 50), a Hellenized Jew and a contemporary of St. Paul, used allegorical reading in order to illuminate the Hebrew Scriptures. Specifically he engaged in allegoresis to preserve

FIRST THOUGHTS ABOUT CONTEMPLATION

the Scriptures from criticisms that they reported primitive beliefs, or trivial, implausible, or morally dubious acts. For example, when Balaam's path is blocked by an angel, as one reads in Numbers 22:31, Philo reads the angel allegorically as the word of God coming to Balaam and convicting him of his folly in seeking to curse Israel. In this way, there is no need to credit the historicity of a talking donkey and an invisible angel with a drawn sword.[7]

Several early Christian authors who lived in the Egyptian city of Alexandria, as Philo did before them, followed Philo's lead using allegory to find Christian truths anticipated in the Hebrew Scriptures and thus to show that the two testaments are at heart one. Among the most remarkable of these exegetes are St. Clement of Alexandria (ca. 150–ca. 215), Origen (ca. 185–ca. 253) and Didymus the Blind (ca. 313–98). When Origen reads the story of Balaam, as he does several times, he reveals what he sees as hidden there from untutored eyes. One interpretation figures the donkey as the Church that once carried the false beliefs of the Jews but now bears Christ.[8] Whether Jewish or Christian, allegory purports to uncover a hidden or secret meaning in a text, something hitherto kept from irreverent eyes, and for this reason it is sometimes referred to as "mystical reading." It is easy enough to see how, from this basis, there grew up from late antiquity to modernity a vocabulary that includes expressions such as "mystical explanations," "mystical reasons," "mystical symbolism," "mystical revelation," even *le moulin mystique*, which represents Christ as the mill that grinds the Old Testament into the New. Take mystical revelation as an example. The author traditionally known as Jean-Pierre de Caussade (d. 1751), who most likely follows the teaching of François de Sales (1567–1622), for

FIRST THOUGHTS ABOUT CONTEMPLATION

whom God has two wills, suggests that there are two modes of revelation. One is "declared revelation," which is publicly available in the Scriptures and to which all should subscribe, and the other is given in the paradoxical expression "mystical revelation," which is hidden in each and every moment of time, and that God permits the faithful to receive but only if they completely abandon themselves to divine providence.[9]

We can readily see that Philo Judaeus, Pseudo-Dionysius, Origen, and Jean-Pierre de Caussade, along with others I have named in the last few pages, are diversely oriented to the beholding of God. They are not solely interested in trying to understand Scripture as one might wish to know a poem, play, or story in compelling detail. Philo is plainly committed to exacting intellectual attention to Torah. The Christians all seek union with the deity who is revealed in Scripture. For Origen, say, the intellectual nature of this union appears to be foregrounded—he wishes to join himself to eternal Wisdom—but one should not thereby suppose that there is no affective dimension to his quest. Like many in the late antique world, Origen was discreet about his personal feelings in his writings. For de Caussade, however, there can be no question that his treatise shows passionate love for the Trinity as well as intellectual concerns: he bursts into ardent prayer from time to time. And yet, when we hear the word "mysticism," we tend not to think along the lines taken by these writers. Instead, we usually think of auditions, raptures, visions, levitations, bilocations—in short, of peculiar states of consciousness in which one suddenly feels at one with God, right up to and including paranormal events. Why is this? And does mysticism, in this sense, have anything to do with contemplation?

FIRST THOUGHTS ABOUT CONTEMPLATION

An answer begins to form before us when we remember that the modern rethinking of "mysticism" begins in Europe and the United States only in the late nineteenth and early twentieth centuries. With hindsight, we can see that this rethinking was prepared for as early as the seventeenth century with the rise of scientific experiment: we think of Francis Bacon (1581–1626), Galileo Galilei (1564–1642), Robert Boyle (1627–1691), and Isaac Newton (1643–1727). If we look from science to philosophy, we might conceive of the eighteenth and nineteenth centuries less as the age of experiment than as the age of experience. The elusive notion of "experience" attracted considerable philosophical interest. Empiricists such as John Locke (1632–1704) and David Hume (1711–1176) maintained that all knowledge derives from sensory experience, and their ideas were challenged and set in other keys by Immanuel Kant (1724–1804), G. W. F. Hegel (1770–1831), and Wilhelm Dilthey (1833–1911), so that "experience" was eventually thought in a more dynamic way. It now involved ideas as well as the senses. One interesting outgrowth of this new orientation in philosophy is the development of the category of aesthetic experience. To experience the beauty or sublimity of nature, and, indeed, art, was seen to be distinct from one's usual experience of the world. Another outgrowth is the birth of "religious experience" as a crucial category that pertains to human life.

Of particular interest in this regard is the work of the Protestant theologian and preacher Friedrich Schleiermacher (1768–1834), who grew up under the strong influence of strict Moravian piety. He reacted against it, and yet some of its impulses continued, redirected, in his own thought, which had been reoriented by a new, intoxicating

FIRST THOUGHTS ABOUT CONTEMPLATION

influence: the Romanticism of his friends, especially Friedrich Schlegel (1772–1829). As a young man, and now a chaplain, Schleiermacher encountered the fashionable skepticism with regard to belief in God that had been a direct result of the Enlightenment. The historical criticism had eroded the grounds of Scripture as revealed truth, the creeds were regarded as incompatible with the advances of science, and, accordingly, ecclesial authority was everywhere questioned. In reaction to this, Schleiermacher proposed that religion ultimately pivots around an irreducible sense of experience, indeed something narrower than "experience." This is "the feeling of absolute dependence" (*Gefühl der schlechthinnigen Abhängigkeit*). Religion is not a matter of subscribing to outworn creeds, reading biblical stories that are out of tune with modernity, or following unbending moral rules, as sophisticated Berliners had assumed; it is, rather, what follows from acknowledging one's feelings of piety, which come to us before we identify them in reflection. In becoming more fully aware of oneself at a deep level, one also becomes vaguely aware of what one must call God. The mode of awareness is feeling and it cannot be denied; it escapes all argument.

Schleiermacher became the grandfather of modern liberal Protestant theology: his influence has been vast. There is an echo of him, and even of the pietism that first nourished him, each time at church when a member of the congregation begins a service by welcoming everyone and praying that all may feel the presence of God. With "religious experience" now being a respectable category, something even cultured people could wish to have, it was perhaps only a matter of time before it accommodated a subbranch—namely, "mystical experience." This

FIRST THOUGHTS ABOUT CONTEMPLATION

happened under the steady, if often subterranean, rise in prestige of modern psychology. The new discipline started to find a foothold in science with the work of William Wundt (1832–1920) and G. Stanley Hall (1846–1924), although it captivated a more general interest only with William James (1842–1910) and Sigmund Freud (1856–1939). Attention to psychological states invited people to take note not only of neuroses and psychoses, which were sometimes apparent in bourgeois society, but also in less common modes of consciousness—among them, the experiences of the mystics. At the turn of the century, there come two major works, Freud's *The Interpretation of Dreams* (1900) and William James's Gifford Lectures, delivered at the University of Edinburgh (1901–1902) and later published as *The Varieties of Religious Experience* (1902). The former book shows that psychology is able to explain common if elusive phenomena by reference to a theory of what Freud called "the unconscious," while the latter lectures supply a wealth of examples that show that religious experience, some of which would come to be called "mystical," was far more common than had ever been thought. Ordinary people, not just saints, had apprehensions of the deity.

It is possible to see the modern conception of mysticism as "mystical experience" forming in the writings of William James and others, most notably in Friedrich von Hügel's *The Mystical Element of Religion* (1909), Evelyn Underhill's *Mysticism* (1911), and Rudolph Otto's *The Idea of the Holy* (1917). In the twentieth century, mysticism thus becomes in the popular imagination largely a matter of peculiar events, shifts of consciousness, arising from the direct awareness of God. Clearly, we have come a long way

FIRST THOUGHTS ABOUT CONTEMPLATION

from the meaning of "mystical" in the expression "mystical theology," where the accent falls firmly on contemplation leading one in love into the darkness of God where one might find absolute rest. In that earlier world, and long into the Middle Ages and beyond, confessors were very wary of unusual experiences—auditions, levitations, visions, and the like—since they could come from the devil as well as from God. It would be an easy thing for a contemplative to succumb to pride by virtue of having been favored with signs of divine love, and pride would be his or her downfall as a Christian. No doubt mental prayer could lead to unusual occurrences— St. Teresa of Ávila (1515–1582) is reported to have levitated, for example—but what is essential is the intimacy gained with God, the resting in God as truth, and not any outward manifestations of that loving accord.

▶ ▷ ▶

We have been using the word "contemplation" in an unreflective manner so far, as though it were the one and only word that denotes the practice of loving repose in God as truth. If we look at the word, however, we can see its origins. It derives from the Latin word *templum*, which designates a rectangle notionally drawn in the sky above the northern part of the Forum by Roman augers in order to tell if a military campaign might be successful or if crops would be abundant. If one faced south, birds flying into the templum from the east was a favorable sign, especially if it happened to be an eagle, which was sacred to Jove, while a bird flying from the west was unfavorable. Augury was more complex than this, though. Should a crow call

FIRST THOUGHTS ABOUT CONTEMPLATION

from the east, the omen was propitious, as it was if a raven called from the west. Owls were usually a bad sign, but if an owl called from the east it was a good omen. From *templum* we get "temple," and so contemplation is something done in or near a temple: it is attending to God in an ecclesially appropriate manner.

If we turn to the eastern Church, we will find that their word we translate by "contemplation" is θεωρία (transl. *theoría*). It is a viewing or a beholding of something. The ancient Greeks had envoys called θεωροί (transl. *theoroi*) who would be sent by their community to observe foreign sacred games or festivals and offer sacrifices there. The visual character of θεωρία cannot be ignored, nor once one knows about the templum can the visual reference buried in "contemplation." Christian beholding of God cannot avoid this ocular metaphor, even when God is held to be invisible, incomprehensible, ineffable, and shrouded in darkness. It is one of the things that separates expressions of Christian and Jewish spirituality. I mentioned at the start of this chapter that Judaism has "contemplative" practices, if one takes the adjective to have a very broad semantic reach. Philo wrote about the Therapeutæ, a Jewish ascetic group that sought wisdom through the cultivation of study and prayer, and his references to them in his treatise *On the Contemplative Life* encouraged readers to think that contemplation was and is practiced by the Jews.

What we find, though, is that Jewish spirituality is less attuned to the eyes than to the ears. One hears of *hagah* in Psalms 1:2, which alludes to wordless sounds, like a low moan; it invites one to picture a person saying sacred words over and over in the depths of his or her heart. It is one of the ironies of the history of our subject that

FIRST THOUGHTS ABOUT CONTEMPLATION

Christians have found most of our most cherished texts about it in the Hebrew Scriptures, as rendered into Greek (Septuagint) or Latin (Vulgate), but that the original words that we translate have no visual element at all. It is one of the reasons why one needs to reflect on issues of cultural and religious adoption whenever using the word "contemplation."

In Arabic there is a rich lexicon for words that can be translated by the English word "contemplation," although several caveats are needed. The word *fikr* means to think deeply about something so as to gain a true understanding of it with a view to gaining wisdom about the matter. Other words cluster around our English word: *tafakkur* ("thinking"), *tadabbur* ("reflecting"), and *tadhakkur* ("remembering"). There are words stemming from the root *nūn ẓā rā* that refer to the gaze, but these tend to revolve around the moral dangers of curiosity or the perpetuation of the male gaze. The Sufis recur to a visual lexicon when evoking Allah, perhaps especially in seeing the divine beauty in beardless youths. A well-known, though contested, hadith (a reported saying) has Muhammed stating, "I saw my Lord in the shape of a youth with a cap awry." The image became common in Persian poetry, where the erotic and the mystical sometimes fuse, as also happens in the Hebrew Song of Solomon and Christian commentaries on it. In general, though, Muslims take the Quran to teach that Allah himself is beyond all human categories and therefore escapes effective contemplation. "No vision can encompass Him, but He encompasses all vision" (Quran 6:103). Nothing here, however, forbids a Muslim from contemplating the glory of Allah in the world; on the contrary.

FIRST THOUGHTS ABOUT CONTEMPLATION

This brings us to the last clarification. We need to distinguish specific acts of beholding God from living a contemplative life. There are various sorts of life to which one can be called. For example, one might find that one has a vocation for the active life, to helping the poor or the sick, or one might be drawn to the mixed life, in which one serves others while also devoting oneself to study and prayer. Or one might find that one has a vocation to be a professor in a research university; if so, one would live a contemplative life, or at least a mixed life, studying in one's chosen field, regardless of whether or not one also engaged in a life of prayer, as well as teaching. To be sure, if one did not live a prayerful life one would be unlikely to have a moment of simple intuition of God. But one could nonetheless pursue one or another mode of contemplation, including the aesthetic and the natural.

Finally, one might discover that one has a vocation to a contemplative religious order, such as the Carmelites, Cistercians, or Carthusians, in which case one's entire life will be devoted to study and prayer, along with work as assigned for the well-being of the community. Contemplation is usually preceded and shaped by a commitment to one or another institution or tradition. After entering the order and having learned its ways, one might live out one's entire vocation and perhaps have just one moment of simple intuition of God, and that single instant would justify an entire life of reclusion. Yet much of that life would be devoted to searching the Scriptures, reading commentaries and theology, engaging in mental prayer, as well as praying the office and attending mass. One would have lived a vibrant, contemplative life.

2
Questions of Practice and Cognition

In the previous chapter I distinguished meditation from contemplation. In Christianity, at least, meditation takes as its ostensive object one or more sacred images. They may be visual, like icons, or they may be written, as biblical stories and poems are. You might use the same visual image for weeks or months, although you will probably vary short narratives, proverbs, or lyrical verses from one or another biblical book over a comparable stretch of time. At the rate of two or three verses a day, it may take up to two months to read the Canticle, which runs only to eight chapters. The image, story, or poem serves to focus attention, and meditating on it allows you both to enter more fully into it, by projecting yourself into the scene, and to range back and forth to related images or stories or poems in the tradition. If you meditate on an icon, you will sense after a while that the eyes of the Virgin, the Christ, or a saint are looking at you. It is as though perspective has suddenly been inverted: now you are the one on whom a gaze steadily settles. The experience can be unnerving, for you may suppose that the eyes are searching deep within you, and that you are being asked to change your life. You might feel convicted of wrongdoing or at least of taking inadequate care of yourself and others; you will probably register a distinct disquiet that you need to transform your heart and mind about something or many things. More positively, you might also become aware of being consoled or encouraged in what you are doing in life.

Meditation encourages mute reflection on a scene and its significance. You look at the Virgin and Child and feel the warmth of their intimacy and also, to be sure, all that will come of it: the suffering of both child and mother in time to come. You reflect on the mystery of the incarnation, how our redemption occurs by Jesus being born, and you ponder the mystery of suffering—how it is that, merely by bearing him, Mary gives her son the potential to undergo horrific pain. If you are praying in a church, you might reach up and touch the frame of the icon: meditation usually has sensual moments, and, when the mind is concentrating on the spiritual, even brushing against wood or metal can seem extraordinary and intense. If praying at home, you might become aware of the fabric on the chair in which you are sitting or the mat beneath your feet. You know that God transcends the wood, metal, or fabric, as well as the image, story, or poem, and yet you will acknowledge the divine presence that suffuses all these things, "in a way without a way," as more than one Christian contemplative has put it. If you read a short passage of Scripture, you can also imaginatively enter the scene that is described. You can become an unnamed and unnoticed onlooker or adopt the perspective of first one person and then another in the image, story, or poem until you have

QUESTIONS OF PRACTICE AND COGNITION

taken up all the perspectives that are available. In this way, you do not simply hear the story in the mind's ear, for you have become a part of it. You begin to feel and think what it must have been like for the Virgin, the Child, or the saint to be in that situation, and you gain a sense of the lightness or weight it had for them and then apply it to yourself.

After a while meditation will take on a life of its own. You might be led, as though by an invisible hand, to other scenes in Scripture and far elsewhere, right into the weeds of your own life. The image or the story might well prompt reflection on past acts, or what you are to do later in the day, or it might even encourage a change in priorities over the coming years. After a spell, the meditation ends; you have mentally crossed the image this way and that, backward and forward, up and down, and, for the time being, you have done all that you can do. Yet the image, story, or poem continues to live in your mind, and much that has been considered remains, still giving food for thought. You chew on what has been given for your nourishment, and only slowly, if at all, is it digested. There might be a moment of understanding much later in the day or on a later day or even years hence. The image, story, or poem marinates in the mind as the hours and days go by, and as it does so the mind takes on something of its flavor. People who meditate each morning will often say that the twenty minutes or so they devote to it changes the character of the whole day, just as a dash of salt seasons an entire dish.

If you pass from meditation to contemplation, you will certainly notice a difference. You will shift from attending to an image, story, or poem to having nothing other than God before you. It can be a troubling experience, like

QUESTIONS OF PRACTICE AND COGNITION

leaving a safe harbor and venturing onto a deep ocean that can take you far away. Many people will need, at least at first, a focal point for the contemplation: a crucifix or a candle. Almost everyone always requires a short word, usually of two syllables, to murmur, like "Jesus" or "Father" to keep the mind and heart on track. Slowly, your breath will begin to harmonize with your heartbeat; you slow down, approaching your center where the image of God abides, and you entrust yourself only to him. Inevitably, other thoughts and feelings come as distractions, and the chosen word is used gently to usher them away. In meditation you might silently converse with one of the persons in an icon, a story, or a poem; you might pray to the Christ, the Virgin, a saint, or an angel, and some of these unvoiced prayers are likely to be petitions. When contemplating, though, you will not pray in words, and you will not ask God for anything, as in petitionary prayer. Instead, you will rest secure in his truth, in his mercy and in his love, and all your prayer might be no more than a sigh of thankfulness. You will listen for what Elijah once heard: the "still small voice" (1 Kgs. 19:12). There is a time for petition, a time for meditation, and also a time for contemplation, for simply being with God. Believers hope to spend eternity with God, and contemplation is a pledge of that hope.

It would be very misleading not to point out that when believers meditate or contemplate they must carefully prepare to do so. You enter a room where you are unlikely to be disturbed, switch off the cellphone and laptop, and dim the light. You make the sign of the cross, not just out of habit or piety but because you are accepting whatever sufferings might come your way simply by being a follower of Jesus. You slowly say the "Our Father," tasting each word, in order to orient yourself to the one whom Jesus calls his father, and, in doing so, your heartbeat begins to slow down, you become conscious of your breathing, and they gradually fall into step together. You offer your will to God, for no one can truly call God "Father" without accepting his rule. Unless you prepare with care, the meditation or contemplation will be aimless; each involves, as we shall see, one or more modes of cognition, and each is also a deepening of a relationship. The mental activity, even if it seems minimal, attunes one to the deity, but you are entering into the presence of another person, the one who is called "Lord," and it must be done with all due awe, respect, and openness. Similarly, when the meditation or contemplation comes to an end, usually after twenty minutes or so, you prepare for the event. You say the "Our Father" again, very slowly, almost as though it speaks of its own accord from deep within, and you cross yourself once more. For the whole span of time you have set yourself apart you have not only been wrapped in the cross but also turned toward the hope of resurrection. For you have been with the sole person in the cosmos who is master of death and life, not just in general but in your particular case. Throughout the day you sense, just beneath the surface of consciousness, a beneficial watchfulness, a guarding of the heart and mind against anything that would be displeasing to God, to whom you have been close, even for a short time and even if no special sense of him has been had. You must not expect to feel anything special.

I have just described, in a cursory way, how meditation and contemplation optimally seem to believers. Of course, not all days will be quite as easy, either when beginning the discipline or even when one has advanced far into it.

QUESTIONS OF PRACTICE AND COGNITION

Some meditations work better than others at specific times; sometimes you will meet rough patches of resistance in your heart or mind; sometimes you will undergo weeks of drought when the whole activity seems completely pointless, even detrimental to one's discipleship. There are times when distractions win: a mosquito whines and will not go away, angry voices are heard in the street outside, someone from the office or from years ago storms into the mind or heart and refuses to leave. Quite frankly, there are other times when you will get bored. Worst, there are occasions, even weeks and months, when God does not seem present; you are left face to face with sheer blankness for the twenty minutes or longer of your daily contemplation. It is worse than being convicted in your heart and mind of having done wrong or not having done anything near enough that is right. But it is all a part of meditation and contemplation. The landscape, especially that of contemplation, has valleys as well as hills, and some of these valleys are cold, boggy, or slippery, and there is no way around them. You can only trudge through them.

The description I have just given has little or nothing singular about it. Almost anyone who practices meditation or contemplation in any religion will recognize most of what has been said and some (Buddhists, Jews, Muslims . . .) will have other things to add. What has been said prompts several groups of questions, however, that will aid us in thinking better about the theme in hand:

1. What relations are there between meditation and contemplation? Must each be practiced by itself or can one pass from the one the other? Is contemplation active or passive, or does one slide from the one to the other? Are there any

QUESTIONS OF PRACTICE AND COGNITION

     other approaches to God that have not been mentioned in the description?

2   What are the cognitive differences between the activities described, if indeed there are only two? Is it even right to focus single-mindedly on cognition, for might they not also involve other aspects of being human? It was mentioned in the description that breathing and touch have roles to play, and the word "feeling" was used as well. Are these things essential or accidental?

3   What does it mean to evoke the "presence" of God? After all, it will be said (and with good reason) that God cannot be present in the way that one's spouse, a symphony playing in a room, or the chair on which one is sitting are present to one. Is God epistemically present in meditation or contemplation? (That is, do we have knowledge or at least genuine awareness of him?) Is God ontically or ontologically present to us? (That is, do we encounter him as a being or as being itself?) Or is there another mode of presence that is in play? If so, what is it?

4   Is the description I have offered, entirely traditional as it is, the only way in which one can meditate or contemplate? Even if one restricts oneself to Christianity, broadly considered, are there no other ways of contemplating? Can one learn anything from other religions? Indeed, must one restrict oneself to contemplating God and only God? Must meditation and contemplation always be modes of prayer?

5   Finally, why pursue these exercises, especially when, as admitted in the description, they can sometimes be frustrating, even for long periods? Can one be sure that one is not fooling oneself in thinking that one is responding to a call to be with God? Are there ways to determine how one is progressing in meditation or contemplation?

QUESTIONS OF PRACTICE AND COGNITION

The questions open horizon after horizon, each of which extends far beyond the last page of this book. In this chapter, I shall briefly attend to 1–3. In chapters 3 and 4 I shall think about 4, and in chapter 5 I shall broach 5.

▶ ▷ ▶

A good place to begin thinking more deeply about meditation and contemplation is by reflecting on a remarkable treatise written by a twelfth-century canon regular, Richard of St. Victor (1100–1173). *The Ark of Moses*, completed just outside Paris in the abbey of St. Victor by 1162, is an extended moral exegesis of Exodus 25:8–40, the instructions the Lord gives to Moses how to build the Ark of the Covenant. Early on, Richard distinguishes between meditating and contemplating, and—following his great predecessor Hugh of St. Victor (1096–1141) —adds a third cognitive mode, thinking, which "wanders through whatever by-ways, with a slow pace, without regard for arrival, in every direction, hither and thither. Meditation presses forward to what it is heading for, often through arduous hardships, with great diligence of mind. Contemplation moves around with astonishing mobility in a free flight wherever its impulse carries it."[1]

What is striking here for modern readers is that Richard sets both meditation and contemplation over thinking, the activity that is most often prized in school, college, and graduate school. As he sees it, thinking is slow, undirected, subject to distraction. Without a focus for our thoughts, they will lead us anywhere they like. When we meditate, however, we are more determined to reach an end, even if we find the path challenging at times. The image, story, or poem that we have before us provides us with an impetus to attend to our exercise, made all the more compelling because we have set a time limit in which to practice it. Most remarkably, because we moderns tend to find contemplation so difficult to do, Richard regards it as rapid and free.

Elsewhere in his treatise, Richard compares the movements of the soul with the movements of birds in the skies:

> You may see some now raise themselves to the heights, then again plunge deep down, and repeat the same manner of ascending and descending many times. You may see others now turn to the right, then again to the left and bend now in this direction, then again in another, they make little or almost no progress and again and again repeat with much perseverance the same alternations of their toing and froing. You may see others again that stretch themselves with the same swiftness and often do this same thing and continue and prolong the same charge forward and backwards in long and frequent repetition. One can see others, how they turn in a circle, and how suddenly or how often they repeat the same or similar circuits now a bit wider, now a bit narrower, always returning to the same point. One can see others, their wings quivering and often beating, how they hover for a long time in one and the same place and by their rapid movements they keep themselves as it were fixed and immobile, they do not at all retire long and strongly attached, as if by steadfastly accomplishing their work they precisely seem to cry out and say: *It is good for us to be here*.[2]

QUESTIONS OF PRACTICE AND COGNITION

When contemplating, as Richard understands it, we hold ourselves aloft before God with nothing particular to do. (He allows the likelihood of the birds looking for insects to drop out of mind.) We can do so in several ways. We can ascend and descend; we can turn left or right; we can go forward and backward; and we can go in circles. These different ways of placing ourselves before God are possible because the deity is not a finite object. There is no way we can comprehend him, regardless of the sort of mental movements that we make. No matter what else we heed, we attend to God, who, not being complex, does not offer us different views of himself. Wholly simple in his being, his mercy, justice, and love, along with all his other attributes, are equally offered to our contemplation. Each leads us directly to him. When contemplating God, we are like birds flying in the sunlit air, wholly secure and yet enjoying our freedom.

For the canons regular of St. Victor, commonly called the Victorines, thinking, meditating, and contemplating are three distinct ways in which the mind works when attending to anything at all, although meditating and contemplating often involve more than just consciousness narrowly conceived. If we go back in the tradition to St. Benedict (480–547), though, we can see a way in which they are all connected. Benedict was the first to regularize what is known as *lectio divina,* or "sacred reading." It has been refined over the centuries, and now several variations of it are quite common. Let me give one version. You set aside a period of time for *lectio,* usually no more than half an hour, and prepare for it as already indicated. You begin by reading a very short passage of Scripture, usually no more than three or four verses from a book that you have decided to read for a long stretch of time. The first stage is lectio itself: reading the passage and making sure that you comprehend it at the basic level of grammar and semantics. Then you can move to the second stage, which is meditating on what has been said, and here you allow the mind and heart to press forward, as Richard says, being diligent with respect to seeking nourishment. After ranging around Scripture for several minutes, you quietly come to an end. Then you advance to the third level, which is applying the meditation to your own life in prayer. What can I learn from the Scriptures? How can I fold what I have learned into my everyday life? What graces do I need in order to grow in life on the basis of what has been put before me? Having prayed and thoroughly made the Scripture one's own, you rise to the final level, which is contemplation: you simply rest for several minutes in the security of divine truth, mercy, and love. And then, finally, you conclude lectio in the manner already described. You have read, you have meditated, and you have contemplated. Now you must let what you have done aid you as you go about your day.

One compelling feature of lectio divina is that it brings thinking, meditating, and contemplation into a coherent whole. All the time you have Scripture both as a ground and as a guide. It is Scripture on which you meditate, Scripture that forms the basis for prayer, and Scripture that orients your contemplation. You rise in small steps from level to level, and, the more often you practice the exercise, the more assured you become in doing it. Note that thinking, here, is not analytic thinking. When you read the verses you are not preparing for a college class or even for bible study at church; you are merely making sure

QUESTIONS OF PRACTICE AND COGNITION

that you comprehend what is being said. Perhaps you will need to look up a word or two or compare the translation you have in your hand with another one, but you must do so only so that you will grasp the literal meaning of the passage. If you attempt more than this, then, as Richard points out, you will begin to wander without an end in sight. For some people, it is endlessly interesting to consider different translations of Scripture, to consult concordances, to follow footnotes in a bible, to read commentaries on the passage, even to compare the translation with the original, but this sort of activity would only distract you from what you have chosen to do, which is to be with God. Leave the academic study of Scripture for another time; prepare your homily, sermon, or essay later.

In modern times we have come to regard thinking almost exclusively as analytic thinking, as defining an issue or a problem, posing a question in a rigorous manner, and then seeking a solution or an answer by way of distinctions. The previous chapter is a modest example. All these things have a place in human life, but not in lectio divina, and for some people it may be a great temptation to turn lectio into a scholarly exercise. If you do not resist the temptation, you will never pass from the first to the second level. Unless you limit yourself to grammar and semantics, the mind will not allow the heart fully to join it; you will not pass readily to meditation, to roaming around Scripture and Christian tradition so as to be sustained by what comes to you. Certainly, you will not be able to pray on the basis of what you have read. God will appear as a problem, a question, a puzzle, not as someone with whom you are intimately related. In lectio, then, thinking marks a very low cognitive level, that of elementary linguistic competence, and when you begin to meditate, you rise to a higher cognitive level, one in which you remember different passages and images, compare and contrast them, make appropriate judgments about them, and engage creatively in role play. You begin to grasp a situation more fully and more deeply. Perhaps your compassion will be elicited; perhaps you will find yourself affected by a word, a gesture, a situation. Perhaps you will have second thoughts about what you have been reading.

Without allowing yourself to meditate with all one's humanity, as a man or woman who thinks and acts, feels and responds, the next stage, prayer, will also be impaired. For the prayer will be effective only if you have subjectively appropriated what you have meditated on, only if the verses you have now read deeply are allowed to cross your own path of life at its most joyous or hurtful. Analytic thinking, when pursued at the wrong time, will cover your vulnerability to God, distract you (and even harden you) so that you cannot change how you live. So the cognition involved in prayer is different from how it has been in the first two levels of lectio. You cannot subjectively determine grammar or the meaning of words; in meditation you respond to another voice, other people, and other situations you may not have lived through: all these things are outside you, and you must come to terms with them, not the other way round. Yet you make them your own, just as you make your breakfast a part of your body. Prayer, however, clings to the subjective pole of cognition, which is not to say that it is self-indulgent, only that it turns on the subject appropriating what is freely offered in Scripture. In prayer you synthesize what you have gained through meditation and apply it to your own case.

QUESTIONS OF PRACTICE AND COGNITION

These days we are likely to think of contemplation as the lowest of cognitive modes, as a free-floating state close to daydreaming. One might come up with an idea when in this state or even a line of poetry, but it strikes the modern mind as very far from offering the intellectual security that analysis promises to make available to us. Not so, say Hugh and Richard of St. Victor, and, even more strongly, others in the tradition to which they belong. Contemplation, they say, is free and adventurous; it is pleasurable; and it accomplishes a valuable work in bringing you closer to God. More, as others will emphasize more strongly than they do, it offers the one who practices it certitude about God and one's relation with him. How can this possibly be? In contemplation you rest in God regarded as truth: not just a truth but as truth itself (John 14:6). With practice, the realization that you abide with the truth, not merely an idea or a theory, begins to have an effect on you. The articles of faith that may have been quite abstract before you practiced contemplation become more and more concrete. You become convicted of the deep truth that you are loved by God, and details that may have niggled you about religion fade away as unimportant. From time to time, you will savor moments of understanding about your life and especially your relationship with God. You have risen to the highest cognitive level in lectio.

As already indicated, no one should expect to intuit the deity in this way as a matter of course; it is exceptional rather than quotidian. Most days you will at best be still for a few minutes in the presence of God without the slightest advance in understanding. Meditation especially engages our emotions, but in general they are let go in contemplation, and we usually touch on only a small range of them:

QUESTIONS OF PRACTICE AND COGNITION

one feels content more often than happy, and only very seldom indeed might one hope to feel bliss. For most people, only continued practice at contemplation, perhaps over many years, will finally grant a sense of certitude. On many days, you will feel nothing at all, or you may feel flat. We come to lectio in one disposition or another, in one mood or another, and sometimes it can be hard to shake it off. Whatever the disposition one brings to lectio, one must learn to trust both yourself and God. We all must learn to be completely ourselves before God, not a more pious version of oneself; one must slowly learn to accept being the person whom he has created with all one's gifts and with all one's limitations. The aim of life is not to become another person but to be the very person God wants you to be, and that can happen only if you accept the invitation to be in a loving relation with him and therefore to avoid sin.

In religion, at least, contemplation upends our modern cognitive hierarchy in which thinking lures us with the promise of certitude. In fact, thinking shows itself to be constrained in this sphere of life. We can study the various arguments for or against theism, and we can delve into books that purport to tell us about the nature of God. There are some well-known proofs for the existence of God, and all of them have equally well-known refutations. The proofs become more sophisticated over the years, and so do the refutations. Some people are drawn to this sort of analysis, especially those of us who have formally studied philosophy, but it is very rare for anyone to gain a sense of certitude about God by examining the ontological argument or the teleological argument or any other argument for the existence of God. Sometimes one can run up against the limits of analytic thinking about God only to be deflected and put on another path to him: the dark road of faith, hope, and love. We need all three in order to begin lectio, but we do not need all three in abundance. Only the smallest grain of each is needed to begin. For they all grow with moral development, with recourse to the sacraments, and with the practice of prayer. They will come to infuse your whole life. As medieval theologians testify, you can gain certitude in the sphere of religion by the practice of contemplation. To be sure, certitude does not exclude questions—far from it. A lively mind feeds on questions in order to grow and does well when it can think clearly and precisely about them. Nor does certitude eliminate doubts about everything to do with the religious life. Many a person is unshaken in his or her faith in the Gospel and still doubts this or that point of doctrine, or whether the Church acts properly in all ways and at all times. A mind convinced of the truth can and should also be a critical mind.

▶ ▷ ▶

When embarking on contemplation, whether as a stage of lectio or as practiced by itself, the emotions are stilled, as I have said. There is no special emotion of holiness to cherish, and anything that seems to be so is accidental. It is important, though, to adopt a suitable attitude before beginning the exercise. I have already mentioned the German philosopher Edmund Husserl, and it is worth our while to reflect for a moment on what he tells us about the many attitudes that one can adopt in life. These attitudes are not the same as dispositions. A mood comes over us, as we say, and sometimes we must shake it off. An attitude, however, is a mental framework that runs deeper than dispositions and outlasts changes in moods.

Most of the time, Husserl says, we inhabit what he calls the "natural attitude."[3] We unreflectingly expect common sense to solve our problems; we think of the world about us by way of sense and use; and we have no use for miracles, paranormal activities, and the like. They can all safely be explained by science. Some people—engineers and prosthetic technicians, for example—pass into the naturalistic attitude when they go to work. It is more narrow and more rigid than the natural attitude, yet it is essential for what they need to accomplish. Here everything bows to "causal closure," the thesis that all physical effects have physical causes. This is not the nature extolled by Wordsworth or Constable; it is the nature examined in physics, at least until one reaches the higher levels of that science. Yet if an engineer meets a friend downtown, he or she seamlessly slips into the personalistic attitude: hands are shaken, or a hug is given, and no one thinks of the friend as a cognitive unit held together by bones and sinews that must inevitably follow inexorable chemical and physical laws. Going back to work, the engineer might have to read a research paper that pivots on second-order differential equations. In doing so, one passes into the theoretical attitude. Driving home, the same person might gaze at a beautiful stretch of countryside, or, when home, be shown an art photograph by a family member, and then one will momentarily adopt the aesthetic attitude. The same person might then start to cook dinner, adopting the practical attitude without a moment's thought about the shift.

If one meditates or contemplates, one soon passes from the natural attitude. It happens when one performs the

QUESTIONS OF PRACTICE AND COGNITION

rituals of preparation and does not require much conscious thought. Husserl is not of much help in telling us how we shift attitudes when engaged in meditation or contemplation. What he calls the mythical-religious attitude involves a passage to a state of mind in which the founding μῦθος (transl. *muthos*) comes to the foreground. This is not false belief, as we take the Greek and Roman myths to be, but the sacred stories of one's community. They may or may not be explicitly religious; however, they will surely turn around tradition, custom, institutions, and taboos. A religious person will see himself or herself as part of a long tradition, one that goes back to his or her holy texts. Certain "historical sediments,"[4] as Husserl calls them, are thereby activated in our consciousnesses: they may be liturgical, philosophical, or theological, or all of these at once. In contemplation, though, one learns to adopt another attitude, one of tranquility, to be sure, but far more than one finds on a visit to the countryside. I call it the "Kingdom attitude," for, in adopting it, one accepts what Jesus called the Kingdom of God and begins to seek it.[5]

In this attitude one enters a spiritual space in which God is hailed as King and Father. It is a strange space, one that cannot be fully seen from the outside; it is unlike any in the world. Here, God is a King unlike any king we have ever heard of, and God is a father utterly unlike any we have known. In this Kingdom power comes through weakness, what is to come is somehow already in the present moment, everyday economic calculation is thrown to the wind, and great events can suddenly grow from tiny acts. In this space where we contemplate God and his Kingdom we are open to the paradoxes that crowd around us, seeking attention. Pondering all this, we might think of the koans that Zen Buddhists practice, since Christianity, like Buddhism, invites us to break out of the conventional ways of thinking that form part of the comfort and even glamor of "the world." Yet the paradoxes of the Kingdom are less a means to personal enlightenment than the embodiment of Christian faith, hope, and love, which include other people, dead and alive. Of course, if while beholding God you begin to think analytically of the divine attributes or the divine energies or anything of the sort you will quickly slide into the theoretical attitude, and your focus will be lost. You can regain that focus only by adopting the mindset that has vanished.

So far I have suggested that contemplation is open to everyone, and, for all intents and purposes, this is true. Each and every person of faith, however small and uncertain it may be, can learn lectio and gain a measure of contentment in the minutes of contemplation that are slowly practiced over weeks, months, and years. This is known as active contemplation, and it goes a long way in deepening one's relationship with God and in granting a more secure sense of the faith. Also, though, there is passive contemplation, and this occurs only when God seeks to bring a soul, usually very well versed in active contemplation, into an even closer intimacy with him. One might ask to receive this grace, but most of us must content ourselves with only what is freely given to all people. It is a mystery why some souls are called to enjoy passive contemplation while others are not. When you offer yourself wholly to God, you allow him to do exactly as he wishes for each of us, and we trust that what he does is always for our benefit.

▶ ▷ ▶

QUESTIONS OF PRACTICE AND COGNITION

When talking about contemplation we find ourselves evoking the presence of God. Some guides to the practice will say to beginners, "Relax and let yourself come into the presence of God." The invitation is attractive in many ways but can also be puzzling to many people and even hurtful if they find that they haven't felt this presence. After all, when beholding God we do not gain knowledge of him, as when we are reading a book or looking at a bowl of oranges. At most, if we are sufficiently receptive, we might have an awareness of the divine, but it is likely to be vague, elusive, unable to be categorized, and without any accompanying feeling. So God does not seem to be an epistemic presence. No doubt people who are swept up in religious emotions, as in revivals and crusades, believe that they feel the presence of God, but it is an easy thing to be mistaken about. If we credit the testimony of visionaries, then perhaps they have encountered God, but usually close inspection of their writings shows that they are using metaphors, and that they are not seeing Christ with their eyes but have a mental engagement with him. This possibility might have been divinely given to them, and it might well have been received with an overwhelmingly strong sense of reality. But it does not quite fit our usual grasp of epistemic presence.

Similarly, God does not seem to give himself to us by way of ontic presence. We do not encounter him the way we do a table, a chair, or another human being. Of course, we usually address him in prayer as though he were an ontic presence, but we do not expect him to respond to us as another person would in conversation. When people say that God answers prayer, they are usually suggesting that there will come a moment of understanding or acceptance about the matter of concern. Sometimes it might be a recollection of a passage of Scripture that is specially apt; at other times, it might be a word spoken by a friend; and at yet other times it might be a prompt to rethink the situation that has been giving trouble from a completely unexpected angle. We should remember that the very act of saying prayers means that we overhear our own petitions, even if they are unvoiced, and there are times when the often threadbare nature of our prayers will prompt answers to what we ask. God is not a supernatural vending machine; he cooperates with us at our level, using ordinary human means whenever possible, including what we can do perfectly well ourselves if we think about it. To put it more theologically, God gives graces in response to prayer—he does not make the problem disappear or tell us directly what to do—and the graces aid our humanity and do not change it fundamentally. We must therefore not expect extraordinary events. St. Paul may have been directly addressed by Christ on the road to Damascus (Acts 9:1–19), and maybe only such a singular event could have changed his entire course of life and given him the certitude and courage to face so many troubles. We should not presume the same of God for ourselves.

Do we approach God as an ontological presence, as being itself? This is a more challenging question since, in a manner, God *is* being itself. In saying that, I am not proposing that God is reducible to the cosmos or nature. Nor am I suggesting that he is a philosophical abstraction such as Hegel's notion of being in his *Science of Logic* (1812) before it is subdivided into quality, quantity, and measure. Nor am I thinking of the subjective pole of this sort of claim—namely, what Romain Rolland (1886–1944) in a

QUESTIONS OF PRACTICE AND COGNITION

letter to Sigmund Freud (1856–1939) called the "oceanic feeling," the sense of being entirely one with the universe.[6] Rolland had read about the trances of the Hindu sage Ramakrishna Paramahamsa (1836–1886), which resonated with some events in his own life, and he considered the oceanic feeling as harmonizing the many and varied mystical events that people claim to have, both in the East and in the West. Having read Freud's caustic study of religion, *The Future of an Illusion* (1927), Rolland thought that a more affirmative understanding of religion was possible: hence his letter to the psychoanalyst about the oceanic feeling. Still unfriendly to religion, Freud proposes in *Civilization and Its Discontents* (1929) that the oceanic feeling can be explained by the infant enjoying the inchoate state before he or she develops an ego. In that blissful time, Freud thinks, the infant takes himself or herself to be utterly one with the breast that feeds it. Only when breast-feeding ceases, and other people begin to appear in the infant's world, and the infant begins to be one person among many, does the feeling go away. When one has a sense of profound unity with the cosmos, Freud thinks, one is merely reactivating the elation that one enjoyed in the womb. Thus Freud's deflation of mystical experience.

If we pass from comparative religion and psychoanalysis to theology, we will get closer to what it means to regard God as an ontological presence. When St. Thomas Aquinas speaks of God he offers the most concise and telling description of him that I know. He uses just six words. God, he says, is *ipsum esse subsistens omnibus modis indeterminatum*.[7] As a first pass, we can translate the Latin as saying that God is absolute; in all ways he is wholly unconditioned by anything outside himself (being, nonbeing, the world he has created, the past, the future, and so on). We come closer to Aquinas's meaning, though, when we say that God is his own act of being, and that his being is not static but dynamic: *esse* is the verb "to be" in Latin. Coming closer still, Aquinas is telling us that the divine being is perfectly fulfilled, lacking nothing whatsoever. God has no potential: his essence is wholly realized in his act of existence. Nonetheless, Aquinas does not talk, as many writers on mysticism do, of people becoming aware of the presence of God. That language differs from that of *ipsum esse subsistens*. He certainly says that God is present as cause in all things.[8] And he has much to say about contemplative persons being oriented throughout their religious vocations to a moment of simple intuition of God. But the vocabulary of "presence," "present," and "becoming present" is one that appears only centuries after him.

Nonetheless, one finds this vocabulary appearing in the Counter-Reformation, and thereafter it becomes pervasive. St. Teresa of Ávila (1515–1582), no small authority in Christian spirituality, writes in her *Life* that "I used unexpectedly to experience a consciousness of the presence of God of such a kind that I could not possibly doubt that he was within me or that I was wholly engulfed in him."[9] It will be noticed right away that St. Teresa troubles our usual notion of "experience." God is not encountered, as though he is outside or beyond her; rather, she becomes conscious that he is within her. Indeed, this "experience" is even more elusive, for as she admits it might equally be that she is within God. So is God present to her or is she present to God? Either way, her consciousness leaves her in no doubt that she and God are, at least momentarily, sharing an intense intimacy. The question fades into the background.

QUESTIONS OF PRACTICE AND COGNITION

Not all contemplatives have been as relaxed as Teresa about the exact relation of the soul and God. De Caussade, whom we met in the previous chapter, takes it as a matter of the highest importance to distinguish cleanly between when a soul lives in God and when God lives in the soul. When souls live in God, they must find their way to union with him by way of reading, values, and ideas. Effort is required, such as in active contemplation. Yet, when God lives in them, they must surrender themselves completely to him. No longer are there any paths; there is no recommended reading and no spiritual direction worth having. They realize that "God has blocked every other avenue in order that they should walk with him alone."[10] Theirs is the nonpath of passive contemplation—indeed, of a passivity that renders them no more than a child who must be led everywhere. Not that these souls find themselves consumed by the presence of God. Instead, they suffer from the absence of God and seek out "the sacrament of the present moment" in which he will reveal himself. This prizing of the present moment as a way into the Kingdom will interest us later.

Before we venture onto other topics raised earlier in this chapter, it is worth our while to reflect still more on this debated notion of divine presence. Let us go back to the twelfth century, specifically to St. Bernard of Clairvaux and to his homilies on the Canticle, one of the most beautiful books of the Hebrew Scriptures. Here are some lines from his seventy-fourth homily:

> Now bear with my foolishness for a little. I want to tell you of my own experience, as I promised. Not that it is of any importance. But I make this disclosure only to help you,

and if you derive any profit from it I shall be consoled for my foolishness; if not, my foolishness will be revealed. I admit that the Word has also come to me—I speak as a fool—and has come many times. But although he has come to me, I have never been conscious of the moment of his coming. I perceived his presence, I remembered afterwards that he had been with me; sometimes I had a presentiment that he would come, but I was never conscious of his coming or his going. And where he comes from when he visits my soul, and where he goes, and by what means he enters and goes out, I admit that I do not know even now; as John says: "You do not know where he comes from or where he goes." There is nothing strange in this, for of him was it said, "Your footsteps will not be known."[11]

The homilies that comprise St. Bernard's partial commentary on the Canticle were probably never given to his brother monks; they are more literary than sermonic. We should be careful when reading them not to suppose too quickly that the "I" that addresses us in the commentary is exactly the same as the historical St. Bernard of Clairvaux. Almost every word in the commentary is taken from Scripture. Even when he says "I speak as a fool" he is quoting St. Paul (2 Cor. 11:23). Nonetheless, St. Bernard himself says in an earlier homily that he asks us to open "the book of experience," and now, in the lines I have quoted, he seems to describe episodes in his own life. It would be uncharacteristic of St. Bernard to draw attention to any special benefits that Christ has conferred to him, and entirely characteristic to draw the reader's attention to how, in principle at least, we are in a position to receive the Word of God.

QUESTIONS OF PRACTICE AND COGNITION

Notice that St. Bernard confesses that he cannot tell exactly when the Word comes to him or when the Word leaves him. Christ's presence is perceived when he is there; it is sometimes anticipated and it is remembered, but it seems quite unlike experience as we usually conceive it. As far back as St. Augustine, the love of God has been described as *modus sine modo*, and this is the expression that St. Bernard himself uses in his treatise *On the Love of God*. The three Latin words can be translated in distinct manners. Perhaps the most telling is one I used earlier in this chapter: "a way without a way," although "a measure without measure" or even (to use a musical term) "a mode without a mode." God comes to us, St. Bernard suggests, not in the usual ways in which one human being approaches another. We are restricted by physical bodies, by needing to use our voices, by being in one place or another, by being in one time or another. God, however, has no such restrictions. He comes to us and departs from us in a manner that does not fit into any of these categories. How is this possible?

You and I are, as we like to say, unique. "There will never be another you," as the title of Harry Warren and Mack Gordon's song runs. Put more exactly, you and I are relatively singular. Each of us is singular and yet each of us is relative to our species, *Homo sapiens sapiens*. The same is true of animals and would be true of aliens as well. Only God is absolutely singular. In Judaism, Christianity, and Islam there is no genus of divinity, for they are all monotheistic religions. The ancient Egyptians, Greeks, Romans, and Norse each had a pantheon of divinities, and there are many gods in religions that are practiced today: Shintoism and various traditional African religions, for example.

QUESTIONS OF PRACTICE AND COGNITION

Some Hindus would regard themselves as polytheists; others would not. Within Christianity, then, God is above or beyond genus. Strictly speaking, we cannot properly use the male pronoun when naming God, for gender requires a minimum of two values. (Christians call God "Father" because that is what Jesus called him, and also Christians pray to Jesus, who is male.) God comes to us as love in a manner that we can only regard as mysterious. We know how relatively singular beings move (we walk or we ride in cars or on trains or planes), but we cannot tell how an absolutely singular being, who does not rely on a body, comes to us. One thing we can say is that God "comes to us" when we make ourselves open to him. We must take the first step, and when we do we find he was already there

If we think of God coming to us in an absolutely singular manner, we will nuance how we think of "the presence of God." It will be unlike any other presence with which we are familiar. It will not quite fit with our usual sense of epistemic presence, ontic presence, or even ontological presence, and that is because these modes of presence are experienced by us in terms of relative singularities, not the sole singularity that is held to be completely unconditioned. As a final thought, the expression *modus sine modo* also indicates how Christians are asked to regard the love that we properly bear to God. It is to be without limit, to be completely unconditioned. We are to love God not differently than how we love one another but at the very limit of that love. This is not just something for contemplatives; it is for all Christians. Only if we love God in this manner can we ever hope to be visited by him, as St. Bernard seems to have been—and if we are never visited in that way, it surely does not mean that we are not loved by God.

3
Ways of Contemplating

In the first chapter I distinguished between contemplation and mysticism. It was necessary only because mysticism has come to be regarded by way of mental experience in the modern age. In some ways it is unfortunate that contemplation and mysticism have been separated. It was not so in the Middle Ages and for long after. In those days, reflection on *sacra doctrina* ("sacred doctrine") was held by many to be a way of penetrating Scripture, which was taken to be revealed by God himself. Because of that, such reflection was held also to be a means of attaining intellectual and affective union with the same God who is proclaimed there. It was an approach to contemplation, not just one among others but the main path taken in those days by friars, monks, and nuns, as well as parish priests and many in their flocks.

In order to probe this medieval idea still more, let us turn to the very start of Aquinas's *Summa theologiæ*. There we find the angelic doctor asking whether sacra doctrina is a practical science. His full answer would puzzle many modern readers. Reading the first part of it, though, we are likely to agree with what he says, especially if we have the *Summa* in English translation open before us. Sacra doctrina is speculative, he declares, because it is concerned with divine acts, not human ones. This makes good sense if we think of what we are told in the Apostles' Creed or the Niceno-Constantinopolitan Creed, each of which summarizes what Christians are called to believe, including some things that seem, at first glance, to be questionable at best and downright unfounded at worst. The Apostles' Creed tells us that Jesus ascended into heaven, but do we really know what this means? Are we to imagine that Jesus started to rise from the Mount of Olives, entered the stratosphere, and then set about finding the Father and the Holy Spirit? More plausibly, could it be that resurrection and ascension are different facets of the one event? Yet if Jesus is fully God and fully Man, how could he truly ascend to heaven? For would not the Second Person of the Trinity, inseparable from the Father and the Holy Spirit, already be there? Jesus, fully God and fully man, would ascend to heaven only to find himself there, albeit in another manner of being, only as God. And what of the Niceno-Constantinopolitan Creed? It tells us that the Holy Spirit proceeds from the Father (or, for Catholics after 1054, the Father and the Son).[1] Since no human being was around in eternity, how could we know that this is true? There is scriptural warrant (John 15:26); even so, this verse must be gathered into trinitarian theology, which specifies the relations of the trinitarian persons and affirms their equality and co-eternality, before it can answer the question. And is that not in itself speculative?

WAYS OF CONTEMPLATING

These questions can all be adequately answered, given enough time and patience, although the last one is more mysterious than the others. Traditionally, the distinction between generation and procession marks the difference between the Father's expression of intellect and his (and the Son's) expression of will (i.e., love). That said, it makes tacit sense to many people today to think that sacra doctrina is speculative, and we are likely also to think that theology itself is largely speculative as well. It tells us a lot of things about the nature of God, Creation, the Fall, our Redemption, and the end of the world, and all of this seems to be one speculation after another. We get closer to Aquinas's meaning, though, if we read him in Latin or at least look up the Latin words that he uses. Then we find that *sacra doctrina* is not held to be speculative in the modern sense of the word ("conjectural") but in the precise sense of the Latin word *speculationem*, which means consideration or scrutiny. The divine acts that Scripture reveals are offered to us to be edified and, in doing so, to acquire a measure of wisdom.

Aquinas does not stop here, though, and this is when we modern readers might find ourselves surprised. He continues, admitting that sacra doctrina is also concerned with human acts, "inasmuch as man is ordained by them to the perfect knowledge of God in which consists eternal bliss."[2] Knowledge, here, as Aquinas says a bit earlier, is what has been inspired by God—namely, what is revealed in Scripture.[3] By being "doers of the word," not merely "hearers only" (Jas. 1:22)—in short, by trying to be conscientious moral agents—we advance in the knowledge of God. We recognize how we are commanded to act in this

WAYS OF CONTEMPLATING

life. We say "Yes" to those commandments and then, each and every day thereafter, we confirm that initial affirmation in our words and our acts. This repeated act of acknowledgment allows us to become more and more aware of God, to understand his care of the world more thoroughly. We might not think of this as a science, for it has nothing to do with either the soft or the hard sciences that we study in school and college. Aquinas readily concedes this objection and points out that there is another science, one that proceeds from principles established by the light of something higher—"the science of God and the blessed."[4] Reflecting on sacra doctrina, he thinks, allows us even in this life to share what the saints enjoy fully in heaven. This is hardly how we moderns think about doctrine, even if we are churchgoers.

So, contemplation is said to bring us slowly to a degree of blessedness without any reference to locutions, visions, or extraordinary consolations, without any appeal to sudden shifts of psychological states. What becomes known in the Counter-Reformation as the presence of God is figured in the thirteenth century as the eternal bliss that we can partake of here and now, and that we hope to enjoy more fully after death. It comes through prayerful reading. Of course, none of this is to deny that there have been visionaries who have claimed to see Christ. Nor are their visions thereby to be dismissed out of hand. Julian of Norwich (1343–ca. 1416), for one, speaks movingly about seeing several "showings" of the passion of Christ when she took herself to be at the point of death at the age of thirty and a half. And Hildegard of Bingen (1098–1179) testifies to seeing many visions from childhood to old age. At the age of three she saw what she called the "Shade of the Living

WAYS OF CONTEMPLATING

Light"; her book *Scivas* has several beautiful illustrations that try to capture what her visions were like. My point is simply that, in the Middle Ages and long after, contemplation was centered on doctrine, which itself was a way of focusing one's attention to Scripture, and since Scripture was held to be revealed, brooding on sacra doctrina was able to bring one to union with God without any peculiar experiences taking place, whether inner or outer. As has already been noted, this union was regarded as both intellectual and affective. It was not enough to have an intellectual regard for doctrine or Scripture. If understood, the words and the acts they denote would stir one to love of God and neighbor. The modern understanding of mysticism seems to remove the possibility of intimacy with God from almost all of us, while the medieval sense of it brings it within our reach.

▶ ▷ ▶

Since our aim in this chapter is to think about the range of contemplative styles that are available, especially in the West, we need to go back to the beginning of the culture and familiarize ourselves with what are now called the "spiritual exercises" practiced by the ancient Greeks and Romans. We can most fully do so by pondering the ordinary word "philosophy."

"Philosophy" these days ranges from its colloquial sense—an attitude or idea that guides one's behavior or forms one's worldview—to naming a particular academic discipline, one usually found only in colleges and universities. If you study philosophy as an undergraduate, you will most likely be introduced to various problems concerning the nature of reality, knowledge, and moral behavior. You will learn how to dispute, including how to draw distinctions and how to formalize arguments; you will learn how to evaluate moral dilemmas and to judge between meta-ethical positions. You might spend some time studying the philosophy of art or history or religion or science. You will probably read some Plato, Descartes, Locke, Hume, and Kant. If you elect to study European philosophy, you will probably read some works by Søren Kierkegaard, Martin Heidegger, and Jean-Paul Sartre, among others, and if you specialize in analytic philosophy, you will most likely tackle essays by W. V. O. Quine, Wilfred Sellars, Frank Jackson, and Donald Davidson, to mention only a few.

In the ancient world, though, φιλοσοφία (transl. *philosophia*) meant "the love of wisdom." To be a philosopher in those days was partly to be interested in concepts and arguments and partly to bring your life into accord with your views. One aspired to live "the good life," meaning that one defended a view of what is truly good and put it into practice in one's own life. Sometimes this meant that one would leave one's home and go to a city—Alexandria, Athens, Rome—to sit for years at the foot of a sage, and sometimes it meant that one would leave a city in order to be free of its corruptions and distractions. This was so for skeptics as well as religious persons. We remember Cicero speaking warmly of the benefits of leaving Rome and retiring to one of the eight villas he owned over the course of his life. He was especially fond of his villa at Tusculum on the slopes of Mount Algibus. There Cicero did not merely relax; like the civilized Roman that he was, he philosophized. His *Tusculan Disputations* are still read and admired.[5]

WAYS OF CONTEMPLATING

Another difference between modern philosophy and ancient φιλοσοφία is that the older word included far more than the newer one. In Plato's Academy, for example, one discussed politics as much as ethics, and many who gathered there would have been politically active in one or more ways. At least some of the students drawn to Plato were intensely interested in astronomy and mathematics, and it is likely that by the time Aristotle was there, he was conducting research into animal biology. Yet another difference between modern philosophy and ancient φιλοσοφία is that our distinction between the secular and the sacred tends to break down with respect to the old word. This is so not only with the Greek philosophers but also with Christian thinkers. St. Augustine (354–430), for instance, revered both the Greek Platonists (what little he could find of them to read in Latin) and Cicero whose long lost *Hortensius* fired him with the love of wisdom, and, after his conversion, he regarded himself as practicing Christian φιλοσοφία.[6] He would not have thought of himself as a theologian, since the word θεολογία (transl. *theologia*) denoted the archive of pagan stories about the gods, which were deemed to be false, even salacious. It was not until the twelfth century that Christians started to adopt the word "theology" to mean reasoned talk about God, and at first there was considerable resistance to doing so.

We tend to think of spirituality involving transcendence, a word that goes back to the Latin *transcendentum*, "rising above." Sometimes the word as used today in the study of religion suggests surmounting a particular condition or state, as when one is said to transcend earthly limits, and, more radically, it even suggests overcoming the self: one transcends oneself by practicing *smṛti*, if oriented to

WAYS OF CONTEMPLATING

Buddhism, or by dedicating oneself to contemplative prayer, if conformed to Christianity. We should pause here, though, and ask ourselves if this exclusive approach to particular religions only is not entirely accurate. After all, one can find instances of contemplatives who adopt the vocabulary of another religion to describe their union with God. Bernadette Roberts (1931–2017), for one, was deep within the Christian fold and yet drew upon Hindu and Buddhist religious terms, specifically of having the experience of no self.[7] On her testimony, she passed from union with God to something beyond that in which both self and God, as usually conceived, fall away, and one lives without self in a permanent now. Here we glimpse a paradox common when studying mysticism, for how can one experience anything at all if one has no self with which to do so? We can find this sort of claim when reading Madame Guyon, although if we look closely at what she says, it is not the self that falls away in pursuing an intense relationship with God but only self-love. Perhaps it is the same for Bernadette Roberts. More generally, the greatest of Christian contemplatives, such as St. John of the Cross (1542–1591), have been wary to speak of experience at all in their encounters with the deity. On the dark quest for God, one leaves the senses and even the spirit far behind. In speaking of the highest relations with God, one is driven beyond the limits of logical language to use an expression such as the experience of nonexperience.

In the Catholic tradition, there is talk of abandonment to divine providence, as we shall see, but in the Orthodox Christian tradition another approach is extoled, and the tension between Catholics and Orthodox in this area is instructive. Hesychasts seek to overcome the ego but do so

WAYS OF CONTEMPLATING

to an end that some Catholic theologians have found disturbing. After conversion and repentance, a hesychast takes up the solitary ascetic life and so breaks with the world and its pleasures, seeking ἀπάθεια (trans. *apatheia*), detachment from passions. Then, constantly repeating the Jesus Prayer, he goes in quest of ἡσυχία (transl. *hesychia*), quiet or stillness, and finally he hopes to achieve θέωσις (transl. *theosis*), deification. This last stage culminates in seeing Tabor Light (Matt. 17:2), the uncreated energies of God. (One cannot see the divine essence; it is held in Orthodoxy, neither in this life nor in the next.)

It is this final step that unnerves some Latin rite Catholic theologians.[8] We remember the interdiction that the Lord gives to Moses: "Man shall not see me and live" (Exod. 33:20). We also remember what is written a few verses earlier, that "the LORD used to speak to Moses face to face, as a man speaks to his friend" (Exod. 33:9). Like many another, Aquinas sought to negotiate this apparent contradiction. He maintains that one can see God with bodily sight only by way of a created substitute, as with the three men who visited Abraham (Gen. 18:1–21). One can represent God in the imagination, as Isaiah did (Isa. 6); one can abstract from material things to determine an intelligible species (e.g., Rom. 1:20); and God can infuse a spiritual light in the mind, as in contemplation (Gen. 32:30).[9] No one in this life, however, can see the uncreated light of God.

Catholics have also rejected the idea of a real distinction between the divine energies and the divine essence, as proposed by Gregory Palamas (ca. 1296–1359) in his defense of hesychasm. (A real distinction bespeaks a separation of entities at the level of being, which would make the divine energies ontologically distinct from the divine essence.

WAYS OF CONTEMPLATING

Catholics hold that this would introduce a division within the Trinity that, being simple, admits of no real distinction.) Another serious rift between Catholicism and Orthodoxy is that the former draws heavily from philosophy—pagan philosophy, some Orthodox will pointedly say—while the latter affirms that, after rigorous training as a novice, personal experience is the only ground of θεωρία (transl. *theoría*), contemplation. In speaking of experience, however, the Orthodox do not invoke psychological categories, as has become common in the West. They answer more surely to the sense of *experiri*, "to try" (along with *experientia*, "trial," or "experimental knowledge"). Behind the Latin is the Greek πεῖρα (transl. *peira*), which means "attempt," "trial," or "experiment." Perhaps the Greek word πέρας (transl. *peras*), "boundary" or "limit," is buried in the Greek as well, and, if so, we might think of the hesychast being brought to the limit of ordinary human cognition by the repeated muttering of the Jesus Prayer.

Differences between Orthodox and Catholic practices are highlighted if we return to the Latinate word "transcendence." In medieval times in the West and long afterward, philosophers talked of the transcendentals, properties of being that exceed the set of categories that we inherit from Aristotle. In his highly influential *Categories*, the philosopher set out all the highest genera and thereby enabled us to describe things as completely as possible. For example, right now I am a human being (substance); 175 pounds and six foot one (quantity); pale (quality); a husband, a father, a friend, a teacher (relatives); in Beaune, France (place); 5 p.m. Thursday, March 9, 2023 (time); sitting (situation); fully dressed (condition); writing this chapter (acting); and becoming weary (acted upon).[10] Thus being

WAYS OF CONTEMPLATING

exceeds all the categories, since anything that is in any one of them can have "being" predicated of it (e.g., being 175 pounds, being pale, being married, being in Beaune). The same can be said of unity, truth, and the good: for instance, everything, in any category, is unified.

Aquinas elaborates an influential theory of the transcendentals as the divine names. God is truth and goodness, because truth and goodness exceed all the categories and apply eminently to God. (They also name particular perfections that God enjoys—namely, truth of intellect and moral goodness.) It is instructive to see how Aquinas describes God at the start of the *Summa theologiæ*. He says that he is simple, good, perfect, immutable, eternal, one, and so on, but he does not use the word "transcendent" when describing the deity. To be sure, if you read Aquinas in English, you will find the word appearing from time to time, as when, talking of God, he speaks of "the transcendence of His excelling power." But nothing quite like our modern word "transcendence" is found in the Latin, which merely says, *per altitudinem, excellentiam virtutis super omnia*.[11] It is not unreasonable to render *super omnia* by using the word "transcendence," although it assimilates Aquinas's view to a style of thinking that he would have found odd.

Only with Immanuel Kant (1724–1804) was the word "transcend" used to denote something beyond the world of sense, and this, for him, is the noumenal world, of things as they really are. The noumenal escapes all theoretical discourse because our minds are not structured so as to engage with it. We do far better with phenomena because we can experience them. So, for Kant, we cannot speak theoretically of the soul or God, a claim that includes

WAYS OF CONTEMPLATING

denying there can be a compelling proof of God's existence; we can only apprehend the deity, as it were, in and through moral action. After Kant, in the era of Romanticism and thereafter, it has become common to speak of God transcending the world, of mystics experiencing the transcendent deity, and even of friends and relations transcending their passing troubles (it has also become accepted to use the duality transcendence and immanence, which arises with Kant).[12] We can understand the ancient spiritual exercises only if we set aside the word "transcendence" and all that comes in its train, especially any of its Christian or mystical associations. The ancients were more modest; they wished only to transform themselves so that they could get by in life as well as they possibly could.

▶ ▷ ▶

Spiritual exercises were advocated by various philosophical schools, including the Epicureans, the Platonists, and the Stoics. Common to all the exercises is the aim of transforming the self—one's whole being, not just oneself as a moral agent—by practicing highly coded methods of attending to it. It is likely that once there were handbooks of these exercises for everyday use; if so, they have all been lost, and we are aware of the practices described there only through quotations in extant works and the few other sources that have survived. Epicureans would gravitate to one or another book by Epicurus (341–270 BC), all of which have been lost, apart from three letters. Later, Romans would read the great Epicurean poem of Lucretius (ca. 99–ca. 55 BC), *De rerum natura*. Greek Stoics would incline to Epictetus (ca. 50–ca. 135) whose thought has come down to

WAYS OF CONTEMPLATING

us only by way of transcripts of his conversation and anthologies of his writings (such as Arrian's compilation of the *Enchiridion*). Roman Stoics would learn from the letters of Seneca the Younger (4 BC–65 AD) and the *Meditations* of Marcus Aurelius (121–80). Platonists would, of course, have the early, less challenging, dialogues of Plato (ca. 428–ca. 348 BC), such as the *Alcibiades*, although its authenticity has since been impugned. We might say that it was Socrates, admired by Platonists and Stoics alike, who brought philosophy vividly into the ἀγορά (transl. *agora*), "marketplace," and tuned it to the problems of daily life.

It is generally known that the Greeks were deeply impressed by the injunction of the Delphic oracle, "Know thyself," and also that, for Socrates, the philosophical life is essentially a practice for death. The thoughtful and virtuous man has no fear of death, since it might turn out to be beneficial rather than evil, and one learns to live virtuously by thinking narrowly about how one acts and does not act. Less well known, however, are a number of particular ways in which the Greeks, and later the Romans, sought to transform themselves so as to cope with adversity and eventually with mortality. Care of oneself applied to all aspects of life. Thus one was advised to restrain oneself in diet, to eat only simple foods, and physical exercise was strongly approved. Running through all the mental exercises is the idea of an inner dialogue. This is not a dialogue of the sort with which we are familiar by reading Plato's *Meno, Republic, Theaetetus*, or *Parmenides*; in fact, the exercises resist any movement toward the abstract and insist on the concrete case of the particular person. We can see this plainly if we read Marcus Aurelius: the book we call

WAYS OF CONTEMPLATING

Meditations is actually called Τὰ εἰς ἑαυτόν [transl. *Ta eis heauton*], which means, roughly, "To himself." If someone wants to attain a degree of composure in life, even some delight in the world, then one must deliberately choose these things. One must commit oneself to a philosophical life. Put otherwise, φιλοσοφία is a way of life.[13] An inner dialogue might involve you responding to a bewitching desire or an affliction, real or imaginary, to see how you might creditably deal with it. The more you are prepared for something alluring or adverse, the more likely you are to be able to modify its effect or even to deflect it. And if you can do nothing at all about it, then at least you can console yourself that you could not have changed what has happened.

Premeditation, then, is a way of coping with an uncertain future. Another way of doing the same thing is to engage in physical definition. In order to come to terms with something undesirable, it helps to describe it as objectively as possible and in a detailed manner. Attaching values to what is conceived should be avoided at all costs. They are human, subjective, and are best kept far away from what is being imagined. After performing this exercise, you usually notice that at least a partial indifference has been gained; there is no more inordinate desire for or anxiety over the imagined event or thing. Overflight, also, serves a similar purpose. Here, you imagine that someone else is looking down at something favorable or unfavorable that is happening to you. This might console you with the thought that the event does not matter: if it is enjoyable, it is a passing pleasure, after all, and if it is unpleasant, then it, too, is only insignificant when one accepts the big picture. The aim of overflight, though, is not to reduce the value of life but, rather, to enhance it. In adopting a third-person view from above, you recognize all the more forcefully that you are exactly where you are, faced with what you are faced with, and that you and only you can experience this episode, which you should do as richly as possible.

Stoics also favored paying close attention to the present moment. To live in the past is useless: it is over and done with, nothing can change it. To live in constant apprehension of the future is also pointless: it has not come yet, and it may come otherwise than is imagined. Better, then, to live in the present, and this requires you not to drift though the day, to have your mind half on the task in hand while stewing about some other matter. Only if you are finely aware of how you are acting, especially if you are acting badly, can you ever hope to improve in time to come. Decisions are taken in the present, not the past or the future. Similarly, only if you are narrowly aware of things happening around you can you reconcile yourself to your inability to change them. You might not be able to control your mother's bad temper, for example, but you can learn how not to be quite so affected by it. Attending closely to the present moment will not always ameliorate your circumstances, Stoics admit, but the practice should never be abandoned, since, if undertaken seriously, it will invariably improve your zest for life overall.

Attention to the present moment is also a strong motif in Buddhist meditation. Both Stoics and Buddhists are intensely alert to the thought that life is more vivid, more precious, more fully lived, if we have our antennae out each hour of the day. "Don't forget to live!" declared Goethe (1749–1832), who himself practiced spiritual exercises.[14] All too easily you can go through a day and, in the evening, wonder what on earth you actually did in it. We can see more in this line by going back many centuries before Goethe. The Roman poet Horace (65–8 BC) addressed a poem, "Ode 1:11," to a woman called Leuconoe, who may or may not have been real, and advised her there how best to live. *Carpe diem,* he said, in an expression that has gone down the centuries. Horace was influenced by both Epicureanism and Stoicism, and we might see the two deep philosophical currents converging for a moment in those two words. They are usually translated as "Seize the day," but a far better rendering would be "Pluck the day." Savor what is offered, for each day is like a blossom or a ripe fruit. Take care not to miss what is really happening; enjoy what you have around you while you have it, since the future might very well take it away from you without the slightest notice. The blossom will fade; the fruit will rot. But do not be hasty or greedy in your enjoyment, for that will detract from the pleasure. The blossom and the fruit must be respected.

Especially in its Buddhist form, the recommendation to "attend to the present moment" has become almost a mantra in North America. No doubt it is a valuable corrective to a baleful tendency to brood on our own pasts—our failures, our inadequacies, our lost opportunities—and our often legitimate worries about the future. Nonetheless, we need to clarify the claim in order to see if it has been well understood by non-Buddhists. It is common to think that the present moment is not wholly distinct from the past and the future. Each present moment retains a trace of the immediate past, and that past moment retains a trace of its immediate past, and so on.[15] We do not enter a new world each moment, but a world that has inherited deeply from the past, both positively and negatively, and one of the challenges we always face is how to arbitrate that divided inheritance. At the same time, each moment reaches into the future; we anticipate as well as remember. Our memories are more reliable than our apprehensions, since what we presume will happen might not, or might not in the manner we think it shall. Always, though, we push into the future, as though being made to walk a plank, often with a sharp impetus coming to us from the past. So, if we attend properly to the present moment, we will be able to give the past and the future their due without thereby denying the fragile, shining present moment. Yet Buddhists do not think of things in this manner. On their understanding, the past and the future are mental constructions that impede one's meditation, and only if we become aware of this situation can be ever properly attend to the present moment.

Christianity learned several things from the spiritual exercises; we can see traces of them in what St. Bernard says about consideration and, more generally, in Christian guides to meditation. We can read early Christian dialogues of a Platonic kind, such as the *Dialogue on the Soul and the Resurrection*, by St. Gregory of Nyssa (ca. 335–ca. 395), which would help to prepare one for death, as would meditating on *The Martyrdom of Polycarp*, for instance.[16] Above all, we can read the *Spiritual Exercises* of St. Ignatius Loyola (1491–1556). More than that, like many Jesuits and laypeople, we can also go on retreat and practice them or even stay home and undertake a retreat in daily life. The exercises require one to meditate in a structured manner and to open oneself to contemplation. We are invited to project ourselves into biblical scenes, to understand them from within. The entire emphasis of the program is to see God in all things and to become whole. Love of God and love of neighbor are disclosed as one; reason and affect can be harmonized, and so can prayer and service. A rigorous examination of one's conscience is essential, and having completed the exercises one should be far more confident in discerning the divine call within oneself.

That said, a question remains. Does Christian contemplation have anything to say about the significance of the present moment? It might seem not, since an untutored view of the religion proposes that it looks overly backward to the Scriptures, perhaps even to the early and medieval church, and encourages spending too much time in this life preparing for the next one. In between, it is sometimes said, Christians devote far too much time judging behavior, that of others as well as their own, and the rightness or wrongness of enjoying the good things of the world. The religion is said to facilitate a judgmental state of mind, one that all too easily allows the present moment to slip by. This is a highly reductive view of the religion. To be sure, Christians are enjoined to make judgments about what is right or wrong, and how best to use one's gifts and one's time. Anyone can be judgmental. Being overly critical of others is an unpleasant human trait that is spread more or less evenly over the globe and can be found in all religions. Are there any resources in Christianity to contest this negative view of the faith?

One place to look is the potent book *The Sacrament of the Present Moment* that is ascribed to De Caussade, whom I have mentioned in each of the previous chapters. It cannot be said that the book is a major work of contemplation;

WAYS OF CONTEMPLATING

it derives from towering authors such as the Pseudo-Dionysius, St. John of the Cross, St. Ignatius Loyola, and St. François de Sales rather than joining their number. And a current of Quietism, probably coming from Madame Guyon (1648–1717), that runs through parts of it is a matter to be weighed. A word about Quietism is in order, since it has come up earlier in my references to Madame Guyon. It is a complex movement, one that invites many distinctions between, for instance, the writings of Miguel de Molinos (1628–1696) and those of Madame Guyon and François Fénelon (1651–1715), and in each case one needs to evaluate the complex web of political and religious intrigue in which Quietists were caught, especially in France. In terms of religion, it is one thing calmly to accept what comes our way, to allow God full reign in our lives, as Madame Guyon advocated, and quite another not even to resist temptations, as Molinos held. More generally, Quietism tends to simplify delicate spiritual issues, and sometimes its counsels are all too vague and, therefore, dangerous for souls in need of precise guidance. (Some Catholics will convict hesychasm of a sort of quietism.) "I must not, like the quietists, reduce all religion to a denial of any specific action," says the author of *The Sacrament of the Present Moment*, and we may take that caution to indicate enough of a distance between the spirituality of the book and that proposed by Molinos, in particular.[17]

It seems very likely that the author of *The Sacrament of the Present Moment* closely follows St. François de Sales's distinction between the two wills of God in his *Treatise on the Love of God* (1616). There we find that revelation gives us the declared will of God; we can discern that will in the Scriptures, and it tells us how we are to act in this life. Will, remember, is not conceived in theology simply as determination, even mental force; it is also the mental faculty where love abides. We are to act in response to the demonstrable love that God has shown for us in creating us and in guiding us so that we might be redeemed. Also, though, we are directed to uncover the permissive will of God. For God did not cease speaking when the Bible was completed or when all the Creeds were written. He speaks now, but in a hidden manner, in and through what comes to each of us in the living present. Each moment consists of situations and events, and each of these is freely offered to us by God to be used in order to draw closer to him.

It may be that, from time to time, our desire and God's desire completely coincide, in which case it is easy to accept what God offers. More often than not, however, the divine will deviates from our own. De Sales and de Caussade both urge their readers that, once we have discerned this divine will (no easy thing), we may abandon ourselves to it, and, in doing so, we shall draw closer to God. No assurances are given that our lives will be any happier in a worldly sense; it may be that, in following God's permissive will, we shall expose ourselves to terrible suffering. Should that happen, one cannot blame God for not protecting us: he has permitted the evil so that we might be tested, refined, and mysteriously draw closer to him in love. Even if one is led into suffering, it is said, one will still be at rest. *E'n la sua volontade è nostra pace* ("And in his will there is our peace," as Dante writes in the *Paradiso*).[18] God's love for us appears as light in his declared will and as darkness in his permissive will.

For the author of *The Sacrament of the Present Moment*, each moment contains what it signifies in a hidden manner, and what it signifies is precisely the mystery of a love that is given only if one abandons oneself to divine providence. "No moment is trivial since each one contains a divine kingdom," we are told.[19] For Stoics and Buddhists, this would not be a satisfactory state of affairs, since it would deflect attention to the present moment to a world of religious values that englobe it. The thought of being completely abandoned to a dark divine will would run against the desire to live well in this world. And for many a Catholic, there would be hesitation in extending the system of sacraments beyond the seven ones affirmed by the Church since the Council of Trent (1545–1563) and embracing as sacrament what is strictly a sacramental, an observance that points to God or welcomes him but is not a vehicle of his grace. But for those impressed by de Sales and de Caussade, their words identify that the present moment is always and already divided between the past and the future, and that each of the three is overflowing with the dark love of God.

▶ ▷ ▶

In the previous chapter we touched on Richard of St. Victor's treatise *The Ark of Moses*, taking note of the distinctions he inherited from Hugh of St. Victor between thinking, meditating, and contemplating. I return to the treatise now so that we can better appreciate his complete picture of contemplation. Thereafter, we shall touch on Aquinas's reservations with respect to it and the alternate account of beholding God with which he replaces it.

Like many another spiritual author before and after him, Richard proposes several levels of contemplation.

WAYS OF CONTEMPLATING

The metaphor of ascent is common throughout the early and medieval church. It looks back, on the one hand, to Jacob's dream of a ladder reaching up to heaven with angels ascending and descending it (Gen. 28:10–17) and, on the other hand, to Diotima's ladder of beauty in Plato's *Symposium* (210a–212c). It was also widespread in the medieval period to regard knowledge as threefold. As Boethius (ca. 480–524) had urged, we gain knowledge by how we seek to know something. Accordingly, Richard says that we cognize in three modes: the imagination, reason, and understanding. Here, imagination is the lowest of the three levels; it is not the productive imagination that has been familiar to us since the early Romantics and has become synonymous with creativity. We associate the productive imagination with major poets such as Shakespeare, Wordsworth, and Yeats who seem to create entire worlds out of thin air. The reproductive imagination, however, merely enables us to represent things by images that reason can render universal. We think using the imagination, we meditate applying reason, and we contemplate by engaging the understanding. With these distinctions in place, Richard is able to identify six levels of contemplation. What is striking here is that, for Richard, one can contemplate anything at all. We can gain insight into anything and everything that is not disgusting and, accordingly, be struck by wonder at what we see.[20]

Let us see how this schema works. The triad of imagination, reason, and understanding consists of three groups of two in an ascending hierarchy of being. Now, the very idea of an ascending order of being is likely to be strange to many of us. We tend to think of something as either existing or not existing. My cat was alive once, now he is dead: he existed once, but now he does not. For Plato, though, and throughout the Middle Ages, there was another assumption in play: being is not fully described by a simple opposition, as it is for us, but could be ordered according to the degree of reality it held.[21] Vegetables have only a little reality, human beings have more, angels more still, and God's mode of being is supreme, for his existence and essence are one. With this fundamental idea in mind, we can see how Richard construes the whole of reality. We pass from the sensory world (levels 1–2) to the invisible or intellectual world (3–4) and then to what is beyond even the realm of the intellect (5–6).

Right at the start of the adventure (level 1), one can contemplate the most ordinary thing—a daffodil, say—as an image and by way of imagination (i.e., representation), and then one can go a step higher (2) and, while remaining in the imagination, order what we are beholding by way of reason. We begin to discern the structure of the flower: its bulb, its stem, its leaves, its perianth, and its corona. Having exhausted what can be done in the sensual world in terms of representation, we pass to the invisible or intellectual world (3). Now we are using reason to deal with sensual phenomena, making them universal. We pass from this particular daffodil to the idea of the daffodil and, in doing so, leave the visible behind for the invisible (4). Using reason and remaining within its sphere, we would begin to reflect on the chemical composition of the daffodil, including its usefulness for soothing burns and drawing splinters from flesh, both of which were well known to medieval physicians, as were the dangers of consuming any of its poisonous bulb. Now we have ascended through the intellectual sphere, and we pass from reason to the

WAYS OF CONTEMPLATING

understanding (5). We enter this elevated realm in grace by pondering what is above reason but not contrary to it: this happens when we need divine aid to grasp something, for instance, the status of the daffodil as created by God. Finally, we would pass above reason into the highest realm that escapes it altogether (6): we would behold the triune nature of this creating God who is nonetheless one.

As if this were not sufficiently detailed, Richard adds that there are also three modes of contemplation, each of which is experiential and each of which requires divine grace. The first is *dilatio mentis*, in which one's mind is enlarged by engaging in exercises of attention, even to perfectly ordinary natural phenomena, such as a daffodil. *Sublevatio mentis*, the raising of the mind, denotes a manner of gazing by virtue of which one's knowledge is increased: one might add to what one already knows or even increase what humanity knows. Finally, if one is given the grace to do so and has a burning desire for God, one just might experience *excessus mentis*, the overflowing of the mind. Quite simply, the infinite God cannot be contained by anything finite, including the mind. This does not stop God from visiting a person, but it means that this person cannot hope to accommodate God in the intellect, or perhaps even in the memory. To go a bit further than Richard suggests, we do not bring God into the presence of our minds; we hope to be brought into the presence of God.

So, for Richard, I can think, meditate, or contemplate almost anything in the world until I reach a high level, where I can only behold God in wonder. Once there, I cannot use reason to meditate on the Trinity because the triune nature of God runs counter to reason, and I certainly cannot properly represent God to myself in images. At this highest level, I can gain angelic wisdom, and, in doing so, I can become more than human—or, rather, I can become truly human in the manner that God intended me to be when he created men and women, as the story of the Garden of Eden suggests (Gen. 2:4–3:24). I can enjoy the freedom and dignity of being a created being, loved by God, and allowed to glide in his radiance. Richard's is an attractive theory of contemplation, although it is not widely known or practiced. This is partly because *The Ark of Moses* was first rendered into English as recently as 1979, and partly because Richard's entire theory of cognition was criticized by Aquinas in the *Summa theologiæ*, which is far better known and has been prized by the Church. The angelic doctor also proposed an alternative understanding of contemplation, one that has been highly regarded not only on its own merits, which are considerable, but also on the basis of Aquinas's growing authority in the Church, especially since Leo XIII's encyclical *Aeterni patris* (1879), which called for scholastic philosophy and theology to be revived in all Catholic institutions of learning.

What does Aquinas say about Richard's map of human cognition, and with what does he propose to replace it?

▶ ▷ ▶

Aquinas's treatment of contemplation is to be found in the second part of the second part of the *Summa theologiæ*. This very fertile section of the whole addresses itself to the virtues, to which he thinks all questions of morality can be led back. First, Aquinas concerns himself with the virtues that pertain to all human beings, and, having done that, he turns to matters relating to particular states of life. He begins by discussing gifts that are divinely given to specific human beings—prophecy, speaking in tongues, and miracles—and only then does he distinguish between the active, contemplative, and mixed lives in *Summa theologiæ* (2a2æ qq. 179–82). It's important to see that contemplation, as Aquinas regards it, is principally to be addressed in terms of religious vocations, especially the contemplative and mixed lives. Elsewhere, in his commentary on the Gospel of John, which he takes to be the contemplative gospel par excellence, we find a common assumption of his day put very firmly in place. While discussing the wedding at Cana (John 2:1–11), he suggests that only celibates are called to the pinnacle of beholding God.[22] Nonetheless, as he admits in his early commentary on Peter Lombard's great synthesis of patristic theology, *The Sentences* (ca. 1150), everyone, including married couples, has a duty to ponder God on Sunday at mass and afterward as well.[23] It is a convergence of the third commandment, "Remember the Sabbath Day, to keep in holy" (Exod. 20:8) and the sage advice that comes in the Psalter, "Be still and know that I am God" (Ps. 46:2).

It is within the frame of the contemplative life, then, that Aquinas inspects Richard's spiritual map. The question he poses runs, "Does the consideration of any truth whatsoever pertain to the contemplative life?" As always, Aquinas scrupulously prepares for answering the question by first reflecting on several views that will be seen to run contrary to it. The first objection reminds us of what the Psalmist says—namely, that God's creation is wonderful and well worth our attention (Ps. 139:14). The second one quotes St. Bernard of Clairvaux's book of advice to Pope Eugenius III, *On Consideration*, in which the abbot notes that only one mode of contemplation is focused on divine truth while the other two attend to its effects in the world about us. The third objection refers us to *The Ark of Moses*, where Richard distinguishes, as we have seen, six levels of contemplation, only the highest of which seeks to behold God as he is in himself. And the fourth and final objection notes, without relying on the authority of any Scripture or on any Church Father, that reflecting on any truth helps to perfect the human mind.

There is always a drama in seeing how Aquinas will answer a question, and it often begins when he responds to the objections that are set before him. This is what is formally called the *sed contra*, "but on the other hand," and almost invariably Aquinas quotes an incontestable authority. Here he turns to St. Gregory the Great's immense commentary on the book of Job (578–95). It is an admirable choice, since St. Gregory was a pope, and also since his *Moralia in Job* is one of the main sources for early Christian reflection on contemplation. St. Gregory read Job in the Latin of the Vulgate (and sometimes in the earlier Vetus Latina), and not in the original Hebrew, and, in a manner at once brilliant and violent, he produces a moral reading of the book that at times the original Hebrew would scarcely support. A case in point is what he says about contemplation. One often looks in vain in the Hebrew for what is offered to us in Gregory's Latin.

The line from Gregory that Aquinas chooses for the *sed contra* is this: "In contemplation indeed it is the beginning or God that is sought."[24] In a book as immense as the *Moralia in Job*—it runs to six thick volumes in English translation—we would expect there to be many possibilities from which to choose, and we might well object that this one line is harmonized to what Aquinas needs. This is a fair criticism, although we should recognize that the *Summa theologiæ* is not an encyclopedia of theology but a dynamic work that folds positions already established in its earlier parts into an evermore more concrete discussion. The sheer impetus of the work influences Aquinas in his selection of the line from St. Gregory. The *Summa* is itself a rethinking of Aquinas's commentary on *The Sentences*, and it often helps when reading the *Summa* to look at the angelic doctor's earlier views. If we do in this instance, we shall see that he thinks that the beginning, the divine *principium*, can be grasped only by simple intuition. We are not being asked to agree that we can intuit God in the modern sense of the word, an instinctive understanding, but, rather, that when we regard God as the principle of all created being we do so with wonder.

Our everyday sense of God can be fleshed out, Aquinas thinks, in five ways.[25] From our experience of motion, we can see that there must be something or someone that set things going, and this is what we understand by the word "God." Similarly, our experience of causes suggests to us that, if we follow the entire chain of cause and effect back to its starting point, we will find something or someone uncaused, and, again, this is what we understand by the word "God." And so on. These five ways are not proofs in the modern, mathematical sense of the word; they are formal indications of our average understanding of what we mean by "God." And they are all that we need to respond to the deity with awe and wonder. Now, if we think, with Sts. Gregory and Thomas, that God, regarded as the beginning, is the only appropriate object of contemplation, then we shall certainly not approve of Richard's schema. For he tells us that we can contemplate anything at all that is not disgusting and slowly rise to beholding the triune God. Where has Richard gone wrong, in Aquinas's estimation?

The answer is clearly given. Richard is certainly on firm ground in how, following Hugh of St. Victor, he figures contemplation: as "the penetrating and free view (*contuitus*) of the mind extended everywhere in perceiving things."[26] Yet he has gone awry in not distinguishing cleanly enough between consideration and contemplation. We might say, in support of Richard, that consideration and contemplation were not nicely delineated in the twelfth century, and that Aquinas has the benefit of St. Bernard's *On Consideration* before him, which might not have been the case for Richard. So Aquinas wields a distinction that would perhaps not have been apparent to Richard. Once that distinction has been drawn, however, Aquinas can see that the first four levels of Richard's schema are really modes of consideration, quests for certitude. Only when one rises to the final two steps, when we encounter intellectual realities, about which we can be sure, do we truly reach the proper realm of contemplation.[27] We behold God in a simple intuition, an immediate insight into his being, which is truth itself. Even for cloistered monks and nuns, it is likely to be a rare occurrence, and yet, Aquinas thinks, their whole vocations are justified by just one such intuition of God.[28]

We should not be misled by the somewhat cerebral air of this talk of the intuition of God. Aquinas makes plain that it is prompted and sustained by love of God and neighbor. Nonetheless, it is true that, for Aquinas, it is the intellect that finally communicates with God, and that it does so in a nondiscursive manner, even though it is disposed to do so by the will (i.e., love). In this emphasis, he remains in harmony with St. Augustine and the Pseudo-Dionysius. Also, following St. Augustine, Aquinas holds on the basis of 2 Corinthians 12:2 that St. Paul actually saw the divine essence.[29] It is one of those points where Catholic and Orthodox theologies of contemplation differ most sharply.

4
What to Contemplate

So far we have clarified what the word "contemplation" can mean in English. We have thought about how contemplation can be practiced within Christianity and the modes of cognition that come into play when doing so. We have surveyed competing understandings of what one must do in order to gaze upon God. We have noticed, in passing, how awareness of other religions has enabled a contemporary Christian, Bernadette Rogers, to draw upon the vocabularies of Buddhism and Hinduism when describing her journey to God, even when her own religion offered her similar resources by way of some currents of medieval mysticism and Quietism. The question arises, though, whether God is the sole legitimate object of human contemplation. Buddhists, who acknowledge no supreme deity, plainly do not think so; their practice of *smṛti* is a sustained attention to breathing with a view to finding release from the cycle of suffering and rebirth. Also, Richard of St. Victor clearly thought that contemplation included far more than beholding God as he is in

WHAT TO CONTEMPLATE

himself. Long before one could gaze on the Trinity, one could reflect on the sensuous and intellectual realms and discern traces of God there while also appreciating creation. In this chapter, then, I ask: Can we behold other things than God?

If we look back far enough in history, we can find many instances in ancient Greece of the cultivation of the gaze to ends other than we find in Christianity. But we must resist distinguishing between the "secular" and the "religious," which takes hold only in modernity and even then seems far more firm than it really is. We have already noted the importance of the θεωροί (transl. *theoroi*), men who were sent from their local communities to observe religious festivals and to report back on what they saw and heard there. In his *Life of Pythagoras*, Iamblichus (245–325) calls these men "the most free," since they have no desire to compete for glory in races or in giving speeches but content themselves with calmly seeing what is before them: art, music, dancing, displays of athletic prowess, and religious rituals. More, they devote themselves to gazing on what is most truly beautiful, τα πρώτα (transl. *ta prota*), the "first things"; these are the mathematical principles of reality that guide even the stars in the heavens.[1] It is likely that Pythagoras (ca. 570–ca. 495 BC) was the first person to call himself a philosopher, in the ancient sense of φιλόσοφος (transl. *philosophos*), "a friend of wisdom." Yet Iamblichus credits him with the idea of participating in the Forms, which we associate with Plato (ca. 424–ca. 348 BC), and he does so in order to give still greater authority to the school of thought from which he inherited so lavishly and that he wished to extend in his own day.

Certainly Plato taught that the philosopher should seek to behold the Forms and thereby gain intelligence of the

WHAT TO CONTEMPLATE

highest things in all their purity and grandeur. In the *Republic* he laments the situation in which a man finds himself when he has been studiously attending to the Form of Justice and, brought back into mundane life, must enter a courtroom "to contend about the shadows of justice or the images that cast the shadows and to wrangle in debate about the notions of these things in the minds of those who have never seen justice itself."[2] The man descends from reality to image, and his discomfort in doing so is palpable. An even more suggestive passage about the Forms is found in the *Phaedrus*. There Plato relates a charming story of the gods visiting the outer surface of the heavens, being wheeled around by the motion of the sphere that contains them, and beholding what is beyond it: the colorless, formless, and intangible reality that can be grasped by mortals only if they are philosophers. He states: "In the revolution it beholds absolute justice, temperance, and knowledge, not such knowledge as has a beginning and varies as it is associated with one or another of the things we call realities, but that which abides in the real eternal absolute."[3]

For Plato, philosophers become more like the gods when seeking intelligence of the Forms through closely argued discussion. It is an idea that St. Paul was later to adapt in his own way. For him, the followers of Jesus are already "beholding the glory of the Lord" and are "being changed into his likeness from one degree of glory to another" by the aid of "the Lord who is the Spirit" (2 Cor. 3:18). In a later letter he will say that Christ is the true image of the invisible Father (Col. 1:15–29). Taking the two remarks together, we can say that a Christian can become more and more like the Lord and, hence, even more and

WHAT TO CONTEMPLATE

more like the Father. So the Christian does not have to engage in dialectic to become like God; he or she has only to repent, believe, live according to the Gospel, and pray. Justin Martyr (ca. 100–ca. 165) perceived the transformation that was gradually taking place in the passage from classical philosophy to Christianity: faith in Jesus becomes regarded as the true philosophy.[4] The Christian is the genuine friend of wisdom, since Christ is Wisdom itself. Of course, if one studies the faith, as in a catechetical school such as the one in Alexandria, one will prepare assiduously before heightening one's awareness of the true philosophy. One will follow a preparatory course of mathematics and logic, grammar and literature, before one ventures into Scripture.

Over a millennium later, in the thirteenth century, the age of high scholasticism, Christianity was also belatedly to receive a wealth of insight from Plato's brilliant and original student, Aristotle. Among other things, he had developed quite different views about contemplation than those of his master. Aquinas, in particular, spent much time and thought in commenting on several of Aristotle's treatises as they were translated into Latin, and Aristotle, even more than Plato, helps Aquinas to frame his ideas about God and the virtues, among other things. For Aquinas, Aristotle is simply "the philosopher"; he does not even have to give his name each time he refers to him. We can see what appeals to Aquinas about Aristotle if we briefly compare him with Plato on the nature of form. Plato proposed a creation myth in the *Timaeus* that sought to explain the origin of the Forms. They are inscribed by the Demiurge, the divine craftsman, in the realm of τὸ ὄν (transl. *to on*), that which truly is (and therefore does not change),

WHAT TO CONTEMPLATE

which is distinct from the realm of τὸ γιγνόμενον (transl. *to gignomenon*), that which is subject to becoming.[5] Human beings can comprehend the domain of becoming by using our five senses and can approach the domain of what truly is by using our minds. For Aristotle, however, the Forms are embedded not in a heavenly sphere but in the phenomena of the material world and can be readily examined there.

With Aristotle, we might say, philosophy takes a decisive step toward what we would now call "science." He wrote on biology, geology, physics, meteorology, and zoology, to name only a few of his lesser-known interests, as well as on ethics, logic, epistemology, and metaphysics. He must have known the dangers of making public all one's views. He would have surely remembered Socrates being executed for supposedly subverting the youth of Athens. And he knew that his former student, Alexander the Great, would not hesitate to punish him should he make public what they had once shared in private. Accordingly, Aristotle made his contemplation a more reserved, scholarly affair than that of his teacher's teacher. Θεωρία (transl. *theoria*), he thought, was proper to human beings, although, like Plato, he also writes of the gods practicing it.[6] Only humans, however, can attain the wisdom that derives from θεωρία, for the gods are already able to enjoy what they know according to their own mode of being. A statesman can reflect with satisfaction on what he has done for his community by crafting sound legislation, but the person who gains the most from θεωρία is the philosopher, and it is a full experience of θεωρία that yields the happiest life for human beings. It is still debated whether Aristotle held that the philosopher regards the highest

WHAT TO CONTEMPLATE

god, the θεῖον (transl. *theion*), for it might well be that "highest god" is no more than a politic way of indicating the deepest structures of reality. We might say that even if Aristotle believed there to be a religious dimension to θεωρία he most certainly did not think there was a cultic aspect of it. He was primarily committed to θεωρία φυσική (transl. *theoria phusike*), "natural contemplation," about which we shall hear more later in this chapter.

For Plotinus (ca. 205–270), Aristotle was fundamentally in agreement with Plato on the most essential points of his philosophy, and even when Aristotle deviated from the master his reasons for doing so illuminate what Plato taught. We moderns usually think of Plato and Aristotle as offering competing visions of philosophy; we tend to follow Raphael (1483–1520) who, in his fresco *The School of Athens* (1509–1511), in the Apostolic Palace of the Vatican, represents Plato as pointing up to the heavens and Aristotle as stretching out his hand horizontally. The one indicates the Forms above him, while the other sees form in everything before him. The group of thinkers we call Neoplatonists, though, saw the relation of the two founding fathers of philosophy otherwise: they were at heart one. Much of the work of those who followed Plotinus consists in harmonizing the two thinkers. Simplicius (ca. 480–560), for one, wrote an exhaustive commentary on the *Categories*, the first text of Aristotle that a student would usually encounter in his studies. Throughout the commentary, he keeps before him Plato's reckoning of the highest genera as they are described in the *Sophist*.

Perhaps the first thing to say about Plotinus's treatment of θεωρία is that it is a spiritual exercise. We begin our quest for insight into reality by cultivating virtue and

WHAT TO CONTEMPLATE

practicing dialectic, and, having accomplished these things, we work on ourselves. No better or more moving description can be found than in the first of the *Enneads*, which are the writings of Plotinus as edited by his student Porphyry (ca. 234–ca. 305). "Withdraw into yourself and look," we are told. The chances are that we shall not like all that we see there. The experience is much as a sculptor sees when examining the unfinished piece before him, Plotinus thinks; it too, must be made beautiful. Like the sculptor, we are to trim away spiritual impurities and to smooth the rough patches of our moral character. "Cut away all that is excessive, straighten all that is crooked, bring light to all that is overcast, labor to make all one glow of beauty," Plotinus tells us. "Never stop chiseling your statue, until there shall shine out on you from it the godlike splendor of virtue."[7] In this way, through an act of the will, one can enable oneself to behold the true beauty that Plato envisaged.

Θεωρία, however, is not something restricted only to human beings; it pervades reality as a creative and organizing principle. In effect, Plotinus rewrites Plato's story of creation in the *Timaeus*, replacing the Demiurge's innate ability to make things with the Intellect's creative power of θεωρία. The person who seeks to behold reality begins by partly creating what they wish to see by looking deeply within. As Nature is allowed to say when given a voice in *Ennead* 3, she does not create as mathematicians do when drawing figures in order to ponder them. It is her self-directed gaze that spontaneously makes natural objects. Nature herself is made by the internal gaze of the soul of the cosmos, the All-Soul above her, and the All-Soul is herself made by still higher principles that she regards.

WHAT TO CONTEMPLATE

Because Nature is low in the hierarchy of being, what she makes is weak, although humans are born with a longing for more than she can ever give, and this is why we must train ourselves in virtue and dialectic so that we may engage in θεωρία. The intellect is our highest capacity, and only θεωρία can possibly assuage its hungers.

In stirring ourselves, we are enabled to do more, for we begin mentally to grasp the object of our beholding and to make it our own, insofar as we can.[8] The whole of reality, then, is creative, and it designs an order of greater and lesser beings. At the very top of this hierarchy is the One (or the Good), which unifies all the Forms; the Forms themselves arise from the Intellect reflecting on itself and on the One; and beneath the Intellect comes the Soul, which not only gazes above itself but also looks beneath: it associates mind with matter. If we look lower than the Soul, then, we find matter, which Plotinus regards as utterly passive, lacking in itself all form and therefore intelligibility until it is operated on by higher powers (in this, he departs widely from Aristotle). The very lack of intelligibility in sensuous natural reality distracts and hampers the soul that longs to return to the One from which it ultimately comes. Hence the need to cultivate virtue and acquire mental discipline through dialectic.

▶ ▷ ▶

Taking a step or two back from what we have just witnessed, we might say that in general the Greek view of θεωρία was oriented to beholding the deep structures of reality. To be sure, this activity has spiritual aspects to it,

WHAT TO CONTEMPLATE

but these are distinguishable from the rituals of Classical and Hellenistic cultic religion. We can see that this is so by going back at least as far as Plato. In his conversation with Diotima in the *Symposium*, Socrates marks a difference between what could be accomplished by taking part in the ceremonies at Eleusis and by engaging in dialectic. The philosopher does not need to travel and therefore does not need to be a θεωρός (transl. *theoros*) because he can practice θεωρία right where he is. St. Augustine, who as a young man was strongly influenced by Platonism, recapitulates and extends this idea in the direction of Christianity when he writes in his treatise "On True Religion" (ca. 390), "Do not go outside, come back into yourself. It is in the inner self that Truth dwells."[9] One needs to clear one's mind by studying logic, grammar, and rhetoric and to acquire virtue, but in the end the Truth is to be found by going within. It is prayer that takes us there.

And yet the notion of θεωρία φυσική (transl. *theoria phusike*), "natural contemplation," did not vanish at the end of the classical era. Within Christianity, it would be used to glean traces of God in his creation. Around the year 370, St. Basil of Caesarea (330–379) delivered nine homilies on the six days of creation (Gen. 1:1–25), talking animatedly of the beauty and fecundity of natural things. "If such is the beauty of visible things, what shall we think of invisible things?" he asks.[10] When published, these homilies came to be highly influential. It is only much later, long after Richard of St. Victor, that one finds authors detaching contemplation from God and reattaching it to the beautiful and the sublime. It begins in the early eighteenth century, at first obscurely, as in the writings of poet and musician

WHAT TO CONTEMPLATE

Henry Needler (1665–1760) and achieves philosophical dignity much later in that age in the writings of Immanuel Kant (1724–1804).

In his maturity, Kant developed a notion of critique that we need to distinguish from our everyday understanding of criticism. The word "criticism" derives from the Greek κρίνειν (transl. *krinein*), which means "to judge" or "to decide." Many things fall under the umbrella of "criticism," but all of them involve a decision about value, whether it be aesthetic, social, political, religious, or something else. *Kritik* or "critique" comes from the same root, and in French *critique* means much the same as "criticism." ("Nouvelle critique" names a loose group of fresh approaches to reading and writing that sprang up in France in the 1960s.) With Kant, however, "critique" differs from "criticism": it is the determination of the conditions of possibility for making a legitimate remark about something. With the *Critique of Pure Reason* (1781, 1787) Kant seeks to uncover the conditions of possibility for making valid metaphysical assertions. An older style of metaphysics, which talks freely, all too freely, of God, Immortality, and the Soul, is set aside, and a new style of thinking is proposed, one that would sharply reduce the justifiable scope of pure reason and turn our attention to the sort of understanding of which the human mind is capable. What interested him is disclosing the conditions that enable us to have experience. Space and time, for instance, are preconditions that enable us to have experience; he calls them pure forms of intuition—namely, a priori representations (Kant's use of "intuition" differs therefore from Aquinas's). All of our experience takes place in space and time, and our judgments about it turn on our sensuous experience of the world and also involve a priori

WHAT TO CONTEMPLATE

concepts. That is to say, they include concepts that are true independently of any contact with the world about us.

With the *Critique of Judgment* (1790), Kant first turns his attention to a critique of aesthetic judgment. On his understanding, judgment is conceived within proper limits when it is taken to articulate both understanding and reason. This would be so for all aesthetic judgments, whether of the agreeable, the beautiful, the sublime, or the good. Relevant to our concern is that Kant insists that one must be disinterested when contemplating anything deemed to be beautiful. The pleasure that I take in judgments of taste "is simply contemplative [*kontemplativ*]," he says, "i.e., it is a judgment which is indifferent as to the existence of an object, and only decides how its character stands with the feeling of pleasure and displeasure."[11] Kant offers as an example a tulip seen by the Swiss traveler Horace-Bénédict de Saussure (1740–1799) and depicted in the latter's *Journey in the Alps* (1779–1796). De Saussure may well have been mistaken about what he saw, since neither the Grengiols tulip nor the Törbel tulip grows wild in the Alps. Nonetheless, it is within limits a suitable example, since the tulip serves no end; it offers human beings no nourishment, and a wild tulip in the Alps would hardly ever be seen. One can esteem the flower's beauty without needing anything from it. The limits of the example are twofold. Kant does not draw attention to the medical properties of tulips—to alleviate itches and stings—or even to the fashion for having pots of the flowers to enhance one's home, which had been prominent earlier in the century, especially in Holland.

Two things are immediately noticeable in what Kant says about aesthetic contemplation. The first is that the

WHAT TO CONTEMPLATE

object in question need not even exist. I can enjoy the landscape of Perelandra, for example.[12] Also, it makes no difference to Kant, as regards aesthetic judgment, if I am looking at a beautiful landscape near Nolay in the Bourgogne or if I am imagining one in a part of the world I've not visited. Even if my imagined beautiful scene in Laos, say, is quite mistaken, it does not derogate from my aesthetic judgment of it. And the second is that, in contrast to the Christian tradition of divine contemplation—with the possible exception of some Quietists—the investments of love drop out of consideration. I must have no interest in the object before me; I must not be thinking about putting it to use (e.g., buying a property in the Bourgogne that I could rent out as an Airbnb, thereby referring the beauty of the place to a fiscal end). I must not be thinking of God in economic terms: making acts of adoration simply in order to win a high place in heaven.

With Kant, contemplation is loosened from God as its natural or inevitable object. To some extent, it reflects on the "I" that has been engaged in critique. But, as Kierkegaard observed, "the more the *I* in criticism became absorbed in contemplation of the *I*, the leaner and leaner the *I* became, until it ended with becoming a ghost, immortal like Aurora's husband."[13] More, it attends to nature and the arts and, in doing so, an infinite object of attention, God, is replaced with finite objects. It is worthwhile to pause and consider this. It had long been thought that one can truly contemplate only that which is infinite, since one would inevitably exhaust anything finite over a period of time. And yet it is entirely traditional that one contemplates the self, even one's death, which have their own mysteries. Also, the question arises whether one can

WHAT TO CONTEMPLATE

really deplete a finite object by attending assiduously to it. Some modern and contemporary writing has set this as a goal. Think of Raymond Roussel's poem "La Vu" (1904), which, in over sixty pages, tries to describe as fully as possible a miniature beach scene painted on a pen holder. Think also of Francis Ponge's "Le Verre d'Eau" (1948), a poem in the genre of a diary, which broods for page after page on a single glass of water. And, finally, think of Georges Perec's *Tentative d'épuisement d'un lieu parisien* (1982), which attempts to say all that one can about Place Sainte-Suplice in Paris over the course of an afternoon. All of these writings attempt to say everything about an object, and the limit they must negotiate is how to keep doing so without becoming tedious. No doubt there is always more to see in whatever one examines, but is it always worth talking about? The person who seeks to contemplate God does not have this problem, since loving reflection on truth, beauty, justice, mercy can go on, entering into greater and greater profundities, until the one attempting it can no longer continue. We might see the literary project of *tout dire* ("saying everything") to be a belated secular adaptation of beholding the deity. Regard for the immanent sometimes dislodges cognizance of the transcendent.

In aesthetic contemplation, then, the adjective changes the meaning of the noun; it edges it away from bespeaking love to requiring disinterest. Yet ordinary experience tells us that we often avail ourselves of just this activity and do so with pleasure. We go for a walk in the country and stop before a scene, sometimes for a long stretch of time, allowing our eyes to wander this way and that, taking in prospects, patterns and colors, perhaps remembering passages from beloved authors (e.g., William Wordsworth, Henry

WHAT TO CONTEMPLATE

David Thoreau, John Clare), and one feels cleansed from the troubles of the week, restored in body and spirit. The philosopher who most helps us to think why this is so is Arthur Schopenhauer (1788–1860), who was himself deeply marked by Kant's critical philosophy. Schopenhauer seeks to simplify the teaching of the *Critique of Pure Reason*: our intuitions of the world—roughly, our direct representations of the world as given in space and time—along with the categories of the understanding that filter them, are all reduced to causality, and causality is itself led back to the principle of sufficient reason. This principle has four roots: the physical, the logical, the mathematical, and the moral. Everywhere we find it prompting us to ask, Where? When? Why? and Wherefore? Almost always in daily life we are constrained to answer these questions. But the principle does not give the whole picture of human reality for Schopenhauer.

Unlike Kant, Schopenhauer thinks that we have some minimal awareness of the noumenal realm, and that this occurs in the exercise of the will. If you look at me, you will see my body as an object. But my sense of my living body is very different: it directly affirms the noumenal reality of myself as blind will. How so? When I will myself to move my right arm it moves; my act does not require any reference to an intuition of space, since it comes strictly from within myself, and yet it involves an inner intuition of time. If I wish to move my arm over my head and also pick up a mug of coffee, I must perform first the one act and then the other. My will, Schopenhauer says, is anterior to my cognitive abilities: it precedes my capacity to represent the world, and it cannot be brought into sharp mental focus. I am justified, he thinks, in surmising that my real

WHAT TO CONTEMPLATE

self—what Kant calls the "noumenal self"—is an objectification of the insatiable will. There is nothing, though, in this noumenal realm that I can discern, by any means, that gives me the slightest hope of having metaphysical freedom, of immortality, or of there being a God who ushers all events toward a final good.

What does human life, therefore, look like from Schopenhauer's perspective? It is a grim affair. It is not for nothing that Schopenhauer is known as a pessimist. We are inhibited in our actions by the principle of sufficient reason, and yet we have a will that persistently urges us to strive after first one thing and then another. Driven to fulfill our desires, we are often frustrated because the world does not allow us to do so. When we are not checked by logic or mathematics, we are likely to be hindered by nature or morality. Believers can at least seek religious consolations, but for Schopenhauer this avenue is completely closed. However, there remains one possibility of temporary relief from the collision of desire with the principle of sufficient reason. This is aesthetic contemplation. If I allow my whole mind to settle on something directly present to me—a tree, a mountain, a vineyard nearby, even a handsome building—I can lose myself momentarily in it. I can forget for a while my individual self, my responsibilities, even my desires. I shall be no more than a pure, almost vacant, subject. Yet I will not be looking so much at any particular thing (this tree, that mountain, this row of vines) but shall be reflecting on the idea of what is before me. It is the eternal form of the tree (or whatever) that will captivate me.[14]

The Platonism on which Schopenhauer relies here is vividly evident, at least in its general lines. What he does with this modified Platonism, however, is very much his own.

WHAT TO CONTEMPLATE

Nor is he unduly beholden to Kant: he is not bothered by disinterest, since his concern is with the experience itself, not with judgments about it. So, if I gaze aesthetically at a tree, not thinking of its particular features so much as the idea of the tree, it hardly matters to me if I am in Beaune in March 2023, ruminating on one or another writing project I must accomplish, the self-importance of this or that official in my university back home, or seeing the Dow Jones go further and further into the red. It does not matter, for the moment, if I long to work at another university, if I want a new house or a new CD player. I could just as well be standing in the same spot hundreds or even thousands of years ago, rapt in admiration of another tree, now long since dead. In contemplation, the individual tree before me fades away, as does the principle of sufficient reason and as do my many desires. I am alone with the idea of the tree, which is not constrained by space or time. Schopenhauer goes so far as to say that the essence of the tree "speaks" directly to me.[15] Atheist that he was, his language of being momentarily in touch with the eternal begins to mimic that of a mystic declaring that God speaks to him in the silence of his heart. It is as though Schopenhauer can talk, with Richard of St. Victor, of *dilatio mentis* or even *sublevatio mentis*.

Like many another of his day, Schopenhauer was profoundly impressed by encounters with Hinduism and Buddhism when young. He read about Hinduism when he was living in Weimar and doubtless absorbed the notion of maya, illusory appearance, from what he gleaned of the Advaita school of Vedanta. He read the *Bhagavad Gita* and a rickety translation of a translation of the Upanishads.[16] Right at the start of his imposing treatise *The World as Will and Representation* (1818), he observes that knowing the Upanishads would be the best preparation the reader could do in order to approach the work in hand.[17] We might well discern more than a hint of *smṛti samādhi* and even *vipaśyanā* mediated by his reading of Plato and Kant, although it must be conceded that Schopenhauer's knowledge of Indian thought is superficial. Nonetheless, there is definite value for aesthetics and even hermeneutics in his work. For Schopenhauer is clear that I do not look through what I am beholding, in quest of a deeper meaning than the one that is freely made available to me. I merely look at it, and if I do with all due attention, that will be sufficient to release me from the cycle of desire and pain that he took to be the lot of human life.

Even though a Buddhist influence on Schopenhauer is unmistakable, one must take care not to assimilate all Asian wisdom to Schopenhauer's aesthetics. It is all too easily done. For example, on reading *The World as Will and Representation,* one might recall a haiku by the Buddhist nun Fududa Chiyo-ni (1703–75). It can be given only awkwardly in English:

> Looking at willows
> You forget them completely
> Sooner or later.

But Chiyo-ni is thinking of what happens to prolonged acts of attention, whether to a willow tree or a geisha, not of any idea of the willows that has escaped space and time.

▶ ▷ ▶

Kant and Schopenhauer are largely responsible for giving philosophical support to a new mode of cognition in the

WHAT TO CONTEMPLATE

West: aesthetic contemplation. That it is a cognitive mode for Schopenhauer is apparent, since it alleviates mental pain and grants intellectual gratification. Far more than Kant, Schopenhauer prizes the artist's vision of the world, and in *Parerga and Paralipomena* (1851) as well as *The World as Will and Representation* he offers many vivid observations about the arts, especially music, which he takes to embody the will more perfectly than any other art. It must also be said that he also writes clearer, more stylish prose than any German philosopher of his time. Little wonder, then, that many artists have found Schopenhauer's philosophy of art highly sympathetic, even if they do not always subscribe to the pessimism urged by the philosophy as a whole. Wagner, Tolstoy, Rilke, and Proust are only some of his admirers. Is it possible, though, to extend Schopenhauer's achievement, to go beyond contemplation as a way of overcoming the pains of life and to propose it as essential to philosophy as such? Such an idea of θεωρία was dear to the Greeks; thereafter, it was incorporated into Christianity. Two modern philosophers, Ludwig Wittgenstein (1889–1951) and Edmund Husserl (1859–1938) have revived the idea, each in his own way, although not quite as the Greeks conceived it. As it happens, both were impressed by Schopenhauer when young. I shall end this chapter by offering some remarks on each, restricting myself only to what they say about contemplation.

Wittgenstein's thought, both earlier and later, has been received in quite different ways. For some, he is a philosopher concerned with substantive issues—facing up to the challenges of skepticism and solipsism, and proposing fresh ways of thinking by way of "family resemblances," "seeing as," and meaning as use—while for others he is

WHAT TO CONTEMPLATE

ultimately a philosophical quietist who believes that, when properly done, philosophy leaves everything as it is. Even if we grant that this is a genuine alternative, it will be plain enough that Wittgenstein differs fundamentally from some styles of philosophy that we have noticed. He does not regard the discipline as training us in virtue and dialectic so as to lead us back finally to the One or God. Nor does he think of philosophy as constituting a system that would articulate logic, metaphysics, and ethics and so give us a comprehensive vision of life and thought. He does not even conceive of philosophy as helping us to think through our moral, social, and political problems so that we may live more equably in the world and help others to do so as well. It is by no means easy to specify what sort of philosopher Wittgenstein thought himself to be, especially considering that he wrote two quite different major books of philosophy, pointing in apparently different directions.

The *Tractatus Logico-Philosophicus* (1922) seeks to distinguish what can be said from what cannot while not dismissing the latter as negligible. In some ways, the book affirms a mystical sense of the world, not one directed to what it truly is (its essence as created, say) but to the fact that it exists in the first place. We cannot give voice to our mystical intuitions about the world (or God): we must remain silent about them. Nowhere in this short book is there anything like an argument, such as we find all the time in modern analytic philosophy; it is, rather, a series of numbered statements, sometimes striking in their aphoristic elegance and pungency. In some ways, it is a ladder that rises to a moment of enlightenment and is then kicked away at the very end. To that extent, one might regard it as a spiritual exercise. The same is also broadly true of

WHAT TO CONTEMPLATE

Wittgenstein's posthumous, longer book, the *Philosophical Investigations* (1953), which reflects critically on the ambitions of the *Tractatus* but does not break with all that is said there. We must work on ourselves, as it were, so as not to be tantalized by the logician's desire to prize formal language over ordinary language and to resist being tantalized by preformed philosophical problems: the Theseus paradox, the mind-body dualism, the freedom of the will, the rationality or irrationality of emotions, the problem of evil, and so on.

One way of harmonizing both the earlier and the later Wittgenstein is to view him as a therapist. "There is not a single philosophical method," he writes, "though there are indeed methods, different therapies, as it were."[18] No suggestion is made of putting other philosophers on the couch; it is not psychological therapy that is at issue but a ministering to those philosophers (and others) who have become bewitched by language, who see problems where none really exists. There is certainly no all-encompassing theory, formal or otherwise, that can respond to all our perplexities about the world. That resembles a fly caught inside a bottle and banging itself against the glass in a futile attempt to escape. My task, he wrote, "is to shew the fly the way out of the fly bottle."[19]

In another posthumous work, *Culture and Value* (1980), Wittgenstein writes, "My ideal is a certain coolness. A temple providing a setting for passions without meddling with them."[20] As we have seen earlier, the word "temple" is at the heart of the word "contemplation," but it would be a mistake to read Wittgenstein, early or late, as discussing θεωρία, even in an indirect manner, or even promoting it in the sense accepted by Greek philosophers or Orthodox

WHAT TO CONTEMPLATE

hesychasts. Instead, he is deflating a certain high conception of philosophy, replacing "wild conjectures and explanations by a quiet weighing of linguistic facts."[21] Wild and woolly speculative ideas, stemming from religious, political, or even logical or metaphysical enthusiasms are, as it were, to be taken to a temple, placed in its quietness, and simply left there. To engage with them on their own terms would only prolong them, which would detract from the real work of philosophy. That work is far more modest than people used to think. One calmly describes the world and does not seek to change it. (Of course, when not doing philosophy, one might be seeking to change the world.) A vision of philosophy as contemplative was taken up by some of Wittgenstein's admirers, especially those who comprise the Swansea school: Rush Rhees (1905–1989), Peter Winch (1926–1997), and D. Z. Phillips (1934–2006). For Phillips, in particular, philosophy acknowledges the variety and richness of things and attempts to do due justice to the various understandings of them without intervening or even arguing for the superiority of one perspective over others.[22] At a pinch, one might say the same of Richard McKeon (1900–1985), whose project of philosophical pluralism allows one to reflect on various positions, each of which is anterior to the other.

On a first comparison, Husserl is also concerned with philosophical description rather than argumentation and also distanced from empirical psychology. He desires to describe, as exactly as possible, phenomena as they appear in pure consciousness, regardless of whether or not they actually exist in the world. A pure consciousness is one that has been rinsed of all empirical attachments. Phenomenology, as he calls his inflection of philosophy, does

WHAT TO CONTEMPLATE

not rely, to any extent, on anything drawn from a prior philosophy or science. If one does this, if one accepts one's intuitions—one's awarenesses of things—just as they are, then one will be able to isolate experiences as they are in themselves. Philosophy, here, is not training to return to the One or the Good (as it is for Platonists and early Christians) or critique (as it is for Kant) or system building (as it was for the Idealists); it is ultimately a reflective exercise that leads us to understand how beings are and how we come to know. Just as Plato, Aristotle, and Kant proposed tables of the highest genera, so, too, Husserl offers us a complete list of the "regions of being" (*Regionem des Seins*), which for him means the ways in which beings give themselves to us. For, clearly, not everything gives itself to us in the same way. When I think of adding two and two, the quality of the phenomenon to manifest itself is exhausted by coming to the answer "Four." Yet when I perceive a pear sitting on the table, it manifests itself in a far richer way: I could spend a long time describing its coloring, its form, the shadow that it casts, not to mention its flavor, its juice, and so on, as we have seen when thinking about tout dire. And when I attend Mass and receive Communion, the wafer is received not simply as bread to be perceived but as something holy. The liturgy refers me to the past (the Passion of Christ, the creation of the elements), my possible moral and spiritual transformation in the present, and to the future (the banquet of heaven). I am overwhelmed by the economy of creation and salvation. I overflow with many modes of awareness, most of which I suppress at the time.

Phenomena give themselves to me, then, but I intend them in distinct ways as well. I can perceive them, imagine them, remember them, anticipate them, desire them. In addition, I approach them in one or another attitude (something that I touched on in chapter 2). Most often, I encounter phenomena in the natural attitude, taking their mode of being in a commonsense way, but if I reflect on their beauty, I pass into the aesthetic attitude; if I begin to think about what makes the phenomenon beautiful, I slip into the theoretical attitude; and if I start to think of what use I can put my experience, I slide into the practical attitude. And so on. If one puts together all the "regions of being," all the modes of intentionality, and all the attitudes one can adopt, one has an extremely capacious way of conceiving one's relations with reality. One can work on oneself, one might say, although for Husserl the work was ultimately to become a rational person, inheriting from the Greeks and looking toward further clarifications of science. We must avoid succumbing to what he believed to be the crisis of his age, in which there is no rigorous philosophical account of human being only behaviorism, historicism, positivism, and other truncated theories of human being.

It is important, Husserl says, for the philosopher to achieve a state of tranquility in order to think and write, for the work is nothing short of the contemplation of reality. Unlike Christian contemplation, this activity is strictly neutral. No doubt, from time to time one might shift one's mode of cognition about something—from skepticism to belief, say—but the mental state in which one philosophizes is willed, not graced. Part of this process turns on reflecting on one's adopted intentional state or states. So, although Husserl initially sounds similar to Schopenhauer in some respects (they both talk of essences, for example,

WHAT TO CONTEMPLATE

although they have different understandings of "essence"), they are far from having the same stances. Schopenhauer affirms that we lose ourselves in contemplation and thereby gain relief from suffering. Husserl thinks that if we lose our empirical selves for a while, we also find our deeper selves more surely when beholding something. How we gaze at something affects the essence that we can examine in our pure consciousness, and, in recognizing this, we can gain a reliable epistemic ground for our knowledge of the event. Also, Husserl differs importantly from Kant. Where Kant proposes disinterested contemplation in order to make fitting aesthetic judgments, Husserl proposes that we must become disinterested spectators of our own lives in order to make rigorous epistemic judgments about anything and everything.

The movement that brings objects from out there in the world—this pear, that house, my body—to being immanent in pure consciousness is what Husserl calls "reduction." The word means no more than what its Latin root says, "leading back." There are various sorts of reduction, Husserl thinks, but for him the most important of them by far is what he calls "phenomenological reduction." It is prized because it uncovers a correlation between how one approaches a phenomenon and how the phenomenon gives itself. Our thinking relates to what is thought. If I perceive a tree, the tree gives itself to me exactly as perceived; if I remember a tree, the tree gives itself to me exactly as remembered (even if I misremember many details of it); if I imagine a tree, it gives itself to be exactly as imagined (however I imagine it). In this way, the world becomes intelligible. Notice, though, that intelligibility here is not quite the same as what we can achieve when

WHAT TO CONTEMPLATE

adopting the theoretical attitude. To be sure, if I pass from the natural attitude to the theoretical attitude, as happens all the time in Greek philosophy, I gain what I take to be certain knowledge of the world. There could be no science, certainly no mathematics, without such a passage. Yet, for Husserl, I can shift from θεωρία (transl. *theoría*) as an abstract picture of reality to seeing phenomena as they truly are, and in doing so I can contemplate reality without adopting a theoretical attitude to it. The response to such beholding is wonder, as the Greeks realized, and as many a poet and artist has as well.

That poets are phenomenologists, at least incipiently, is something that Husserl recognized and acknowledged. However, although the poetic gaze is akin to the philosopher's, it is not quite the same, for the former arrests his or her insight at the level of aesthetics, even psychology, while the latter goes all the way until secure, neutral epistemic judgment has been reached. Husserl's student Martin Heidegger (1889–1976) gave still more credit to the poets. He read several who wrote in German—Friedrich Hölderlin (1770–1843), Stefan George (1868–1933), and Georg Trakl (1887–1914)—even though he could be quite tone deaf to particular lines of verse. It is the poet, he thought, who sings the holy word that gathers communities together. The thinker's task is to brood on being; the poet's is to live and write in the difficult space left by the Christian God, in whom, he thought, we no longer really believe. This space has not yet been inhabited by any new gods, whomever they may turn out to be, and we look to the poets to name them when the time is right to do so.

A philosopher can think being, however, only when a certain mood comes over him or her. So the younger

WHAT TO CONTEMPLATE

Heidegger thought around the time he completed his masterwork, *Being and Time* (1927). It is dread or deep boredom that makes one aware of being, not just beings. And so Heidegger rejects Husserl's notion of willed contemplative quiet as needed to philosophize. It is only later that he changes his mind on the topic. He urges us to see that, in our technological age, we tend to look always to utility and accordingly are overly ready to calculate, not to think. Science, in particular, does not think contemplatively, since it is beholden to method. Heidegger commends a way of ameliorating our sorry lot, namely meditative or poetic thinking. Contemplative thinking (*Besinnung*) ponders the background sense of a situation; it composes us so that we may ask the right questions about what is before us and not rely on pregiven questions.[23] We are released from overly tight mental constraints and invited to be open to the mystery of being, which we can ponder in the configuration of earth and sky, mortals and divinities. Indeed, when we marvel at the world, questions of a philosophical kind do not come to us. Only when we are done with our pondering do they impinge on us. Reading Hölderlin, George or Trakl—and presumably other poets—can aid us in this, but not if we approach them as literary critics do: philology, or any literary formalism, will simply trammel us in calculative thinking. We must learn to let the poetry release us from our mental constraints so that we can hear the holy song.[24]

5
Why Contemplate?

There are objections to both the contemplative life and contemplation, and these arise from within religion as well as from outside it. I shall begin this chapter by noting some of these criticisms and then turn to consider one or two reasons for nonetheless pursuing it.

It may be surprising to learn that Aquinas himself had reservations about the contemplative life, especially since he maintained that just one simple intuition of God would be sufficient to justify an entire vocation as a Carthusian, Cistercian, or Poor Clare. For Aquinas, as for other friars minor (later known as the Dominicans), such as Hugh of St. Cher (1200–1263), the mixed life, such as lived by the friars minor, was preferable to either the contemplative or active life. This is because the prayer and study that a friar undertook in private informed the preaching that he would do in public, and so the fruits of contemplation were distributed. As one of the Dominican mottos has it: *Contemplata alliis tradere* (Contemplate, then share with others). So, for Aquinas, the hierarchy of religious vocations does

WHY CONTEMPLATE?

not have the contemplative life at the top, as one might expect, but beneath the mixed life and with the active life coming last. At all periods of history, some people have looked askance at those who devote themselves to a contemplative vocation. There are four main criticisms: it is a waste of life, at best an idle life; it is unnatural; it leads one into heresy; and it is a drain on the resources of those who support them. Would it not be better, it is asked, to have a family, a job, and also pray and study if one wishes to do so? In other words, the mixed life is conceded to have some value, but not the contemplative life.

Whether we are affected by these criticisms depends on whether or not we have a vocation to a contemplative life. If we do, then nothing will deter us from pursuing it. One gets nowhere trying to argue against the mind and heart when they act as one. While a contemplative life should be tranquil, it will never be idle. Contemplative monks and nuns have many tasks to do, in the garden, the fields, the workshops, and the choir, as well as to pray alone in their cells. Of course, in medieval times many people were attracted to monasteries, not always those of the contemplative orders, so that they might have enough to eat. Even wealthy families would send their third son (and sometimes even their second son) to a monastery because the oldest son would inherit all the family property, leaving little or nothing for the others. Daughters deemed unfit for marriage would also be consigned to cloisters. It was usually expected that the children of nobility would gain positions of authority within the community. We should not think, though, that all friars, monks, and nuns took themselves to be called by God to join religious orders; for some, it was an exigency that they could not disregard. It should come

WHY CONTEMPLATE?

as no surprise that some monks could be unruly; some monasteries had dungeons to deal with gross offenders.[1] Children as young as five were once sent to religious communities, although nowadays the youngest age one can become an oblate is eighteen. Not so in Buddhism, even now: in the Theravada tradition one can still begin a monastic vocation at the age of eight, although one becomes a monk usually no earlier than twenty.

Does one waste one's life by removing oneself from society and spending a large part of the day and much of the night in prayer? If one firmly believes that this is the path that God has chosen for one, the question will appear beside the point. God chooses very few people to face the many challenges of such a life—consecrated solitude, penance, manual labor, frequent liturgical prayer—and it must be remembered that not everyone, even in secular society, believes that he or she is suited to marriage or even a long-lasting relationship. Besides, there are people who choose paths that seem to add little to the social good. An artist may secret himself or herself away for decades and perhaps paint only one work or write one poem that will comfort or animate admirers in years to come. A soldier may train hard for years and serve in a serious engagement only once, if that. A professor might begin academic life with zest, inspire students to learn, and publish a revised version of his or her doctoral dissertation only to fizzle out after gaining tenure and then do nothing much at all for decade after decade.

In chapter 1, I mentioned Margaret Porette, who suffered a cruel execution for her beliefs about contemplation. Among other things, she maintained until death that the natural will is annihilated in its relationship with God:

WHY CONTEMPLATE?

the soul "shall do nothing, says God; but I shall do my work in her without her. For her knowledge of her nothingness and her faith in me have so brought her to nothing that she can do nothing."[2] Certainly, there have have been motifs in some forms of contemplation that the Church has suppressed violently—again, I recall Madame Guyon—and the annihilation of the natural will is one of them, but contemplation in and of itself need not run against the teachings of the Church, no more so than can happen in academic theology or even preaching. Sometimes what counts as "heresy" is a conflict between the finely honed theology of the Church and the flamboyant language of a mystic, many of whom are not trained in the niceties of theological argument. Besides, there are more common worries than falling into heresy. When a religious person begins to follow the interior life, one is advised to do so under a spiritual adviser. This is not so much to prevent one going against the teachings of the Church as to ensure that that the person new to the spiritual life will be able to deal appropriately with the many specters that are likely to spring from one's past or present. At first contemplation is a delight, but before long the memory throws up dark images from one's past, and the natural will revolts against a practice that limits its sphere of operations.

An unavoidable part of the process of discernment as to whether one has a genuine vocation to the contemplative life is heartfelt evidence of the love of neighbor. In Christianity love of God and love of neighbor are one: no one can expect ever to behold God without extending and deepening one's virtues by practicing them. Even a Carthusian whose cell is his hermitage seeks to further fraternal union with his fellow monks, usually on a long weekly walk, the

WHY CONTEMPLATE?

spaciamentum. As regards consecrating oneself to an entire life of prayer, it must be remembered that prayer's work, both public and private, is invisible; we cannot see the evil that the prayers of contemplatives are believed to deflect from the world. Friars, monks, and nuns intercede for all the living and the dead. We have no reason to think that they are not deeply concerned about their fellow men and women as well as with their own souls being right with God.

No doubt in the past there have been towns that have been burdened, at least for a while, by religious houses being built near them and requiring material support until they became more or less self-sustaining. This was the case, for instance, when Discalced Carmelite houses were springing up in Spain under the direction of Sts. Teresa of Ávila (1515–1582) and John of the Cross (1542–1591). By and large, though, monasteries have seen towns grow up around them to the economic benefit of the townsfolk. Lay brothers and sisters, though not choir monks or nuns, would make crucial links with local towns, and the religious communities would employ all manner of craftsmen and teach children and adolescents.[3] Carthusian monasteries, which are built in secluded areas, have to be economically self-sufficient. St. Paul's words—"If anyone will not work, let him not eat" (2 Thess. 3:10)—has echoed throughout late antiquity, the Middle Ages, right up to our own day. St. Augustine wrote an influential treatise, *On the Works of Monks* (ca. 401), on the matter, strongly advocating manual labor for those who were called to dedicate themselves to lives of prayer, and St. Benedict's rule similarly made no bones about prayer being leagued with manual work.[4] Indeed, Cistercians and Carthusians have often declined external sources of revenue, even from wealthy patrons. That said, there are hesychasts who are "holy fools," subsisting on casual charity while walking the roads and seeking stillness through constant prayer. Eugene Vodolazkin's powerful novel *Laurus* (2012) provides a vivid picture of such life in fifteenth- and sixteenth-century Russia.

Of course, one can practice contemplation—religious, aesthetic, or philosophical—without joining any religious community. If one does so, in the context of family, friends, and work, are there any serious criticisms to which one might be reasonably exposed? At first, one would think not: after all, what difference does it make to programs of social justice if one spends half an hour, an hour, or even longer each day, in lectio divina, spiritual exercises, smṛti, or regarding a landscape? There are many people who spend far longer each day watching TV, playing video games, surfing the Internet, gossiping, checking apps on an iPhone, and frittering time away in other ways. Some of those who engage in spiritual exercises also work to further social justice in their neighborhoods; others do not. It is much the same with those who watch TV and play video games. Nonetheless, those who meditate or contemplate are sometimes accused, often sotto voce, of self-indulgence or even elitism while others are not. Is there anything to this sort of charge?

The basis of the criticism is that one needs leisure and education in which to pursue contemplation, only some walks of life allow such freedom and such benefits, and so contemplation is restricted to the middle classes and those who live on trust funds.[5] It will be said, with reason, that those who must get up before dawn to work hard at

WHY CONTEMPLATE?

low-paid, unrewarding jobs have little or no opportunity to apply themselves to any of the disciplines I have described. More, they have few available resources to learn about any of the techniques mentioned in this book, let alone to read books of Abrahamic or Asian wisdom. Even those with more fulfilling, better-paid jobs (clerks, cooks, nurses, secretaries, teachers), who have greater access to libraries, adult education classes, and the like, may suffer from undue stress that, quite frankly, makes contemplation seem a step too far for them. And, of course, there are others who are fully engaged in the active life—raising and teaching children, healing the sick, helping the poor—for whom study, mental prayer, and spiritual exercises are simply not vital parts of their charism. They do sufficient good, they might think, without taking on these things, and how could anyone, including God, expect more of them?

These views have weight. It is especially of concern when people do not have ready access to information about the things discussed in this book, as is certainly the case in rural areas. Even the Catholic Church these days offers little guidance Sunday by Sunday to those who would benefit from mental prayer. Be that as it may, awareness of meditation and contemplation, Western or Eastern, has become widespread in recent decades and is making headway in medical schools, faculties of education, and even in classrooms, and, while a commitment to daily practice is required, none of the activities need take very long at all to do. I have known people who practice one or another spiritual discipline on the bus early in the morning when on the way to work. Other people take twenty minutes out of their lunch hour, find a quiet spot—a church, a park bench, a library, a townhall, even a restroom—and pursue their discipline then. There are gaps in the day that can be used, and, if nothing else, a brief break devoted to contemplation will help to improve one's mental health. Many people who have adopted a régime of meditation or contemplation have found that they rely less on alcohol, drugs, tobacco, or medications to relieve anxiety, depression, irritability, and sleeplessness. At this basic level, cultivating a spiritual discipline is scarcely self-indulgent or elitist. It encourages one to take charge of one's own life and it requires no special abilities. Nor is it irrational. It might be the best thing a person can do, if not to flourish in life, then at least to cope better with its inevitable trials.

Contemplation can be undertaken on various planes, some more rarified than others. One might begin to prize the present moment and so to be less tightly bound to what one cannot change in the past and what one cannot avoid in the future. Those in the Abrahamic religions pursue it in order to form a more intimate relationship with God, while those in the various schools of Buddhism embark on it in order to seek enlightenment. Concerted practitioners of aesthetic contemplation seek to educate their feelings and refine their taste; they hope to touch heights and depths that they would not otherwise find. Philosophical contemplation will edge one to do justice to competing perspectives on problems or, indeed, to respond freshly to the world in wonder at its richness, its variety, its beauty. More generally, contemplative exercises help one to gain greater understanding of other people, a subject one is studying, or oneself. They can also wean one away from a pervasive phenomenon in our age: fascination. And, finally, as Aristotle taught long ago, contemplation brings us to happiness.[6]

WHY CONTEMPLATE?

None of these things is easy. Even if undertaken in an untaxing way, each of them requires concentrated and regular attention. Are there pressing reasons, though, to attempt contemplation at a higher level than to improve one's mental health?

▶ ▷ ▶

In order to answer this question, I would like to think alongside a very well-known passage by Friedrich Nietzsche (1844–1900) from his book *The Gay Science* (1882). It is a parable of a madman who comes into town and declares that God is dead. Even if you have read this passage before, it bears frequent rereading:

> The madman jumped into their midst and pierced them with his eyes. "Whither is God?" he cried; "I will tell you. *We have killed him*—you and I. All of us are his murderers. But how did we do this? How could we drink up the sea? Who gave us the sponge to wipe away the entire horizon? What were we doing when we unchained this earth from its sun? Whither is it moving now? Whither are we moving? Away from all suns? Are we not plunging continually? Backward, sideward, forward, in all directions? Is there still any up or down? Are we not straying, as through an infinite nothing? Do we not feel the breath of empty space? Has it not become colder? Is not night continually closing in on us? Do we not need to light lanterns in the morning? Do we hear nothing as yet of the noise of the gravediggers who are burying God? Do we smell nothing as yet of the divine decomposition? Gods, too, decompose. God is dead. God remains dead. And we have killed him."[7]

WHY CONTEMPLATE?

Much has been said about Nietzsche's intentions in this parable. Is the madman insane or inspired? Does the dramatic claim "God is dead" mean any more than that, since the Enlightenment, a great many people, especially Europeans, have lost faith in the Church as the way, or even a way, to God? And what does Nietzsche mean by "God" here? Is he objecting only to Christian morality? Or is he aiming to reject an entire metaphysical view of reality in which God is the highest ground? Rather than try to answer these questions, I would like to draw attention to what the passage says about our awareness of movement.

The experience of modernity that Nietzsche describes is one of complete and total disaster. The word "disaster" comes from the Latin *dis* ("away from") + *astrum* ("star"); it means having to endure bad favor from the heavens or even no longer having any guidance from the stars, those ancient means of navigating one's way across unknown country and unfamiliar seas. Somehow, we have wiped away the horizon, and without that fine line the earth and sky cannot be kept apart. Worse, we have disturbed the orbit of our planet around the sun and are wandering through empty space. It is not even a smooth passage into utter darkness, for we are plunging downward and lurching in all directions, "backward, sideward, forward." Our experience is not only of turbulence but also of increased darkness, and there is even a stench of what we most valued, or so we told ourselves, rotting, and it is all made worse by a deepening realization of personal guilt. This, for Nietzsche, and for many of us, is how we experience modern life when we reflect on it at a sufficient depth. We have no secure ground, no "first things" to guide us, nothing and no one we can fully trust.

WHY CONTEMPLATE?

Since the mid-nineteenth century, there been so many social and intellectual changes that have come upon us so rapidly that we are permanently shaken and unable to recognize our condition. Our great-grandparents took themselves to live in a solar system with eight or nine planets that was somewhere in the Milky Way. It was only a hundred years ago that another galaxy was shown to exist. Now if we think conservatively we know of between a hundred and two hundred billion galaxies (and it is more likely there are up to two trillion of them). We can respond to this picture with despair or with wonder. Has God died because it is impossible to conceive a Creator and Redeemer being at all interested in our speck of a planet? Can the Abrahamic God even be squared with a cosmic reality of vast empty spaces, megacomets, wandering black holes, catastrophic solar flares, and complete indifference to life? Or is God immeasurably greater than we once thought because of the scale of creation? Sometimes the very questions are too daunting to pose to oneself; they are like letters too big to fit into a mailbox.

As if these things were not enough to deal with, mentally and spiritually, our social world seems to become increasingly troubled. The Internet brings much of human knowledge (and human misinformation and mischief) to our desks. We are overwhelmed with more news, ideas, views, and desires than can be accommodated. The world contracts more and more, so that we see catastrophes almost every day; our compassion dries up, and we become increasingly desensitized to suffering. More, we live in a time in which what often seem to have been the tried and true moral values of previous generations are being fiercely contested from several quarters. Preferences have come to

WHY CONTEMPLATE?

replace reasons; doublethink has become all too common, even in university administrations; and people grimly or gleefully proclaim ours as an era that is "post-truth." All of this has a somber fascination, to which I shall return, but to think about it, let alone live with it, takes an immense psychic toll, one that we often do not notice until we have time to reflect on it.

I would like to set beside Nietzsche's bleak parable a short passage from *The Divine Names*, composed by the Pseudo-Dionysius, most likely in the early sixth century. It is also about movement, and it has been behind much of what I have been saying in this book. Just before my quotation begins, Pseudo-Dionysius has been speaking of how the angels move. Then he turns to consider the motions of the soul, which are similar, though not quite the same because of how we differ from the angels:

> The circular motion of the soul is both entrance into itself of those which are outside it and the uniform convolution of its intellectual powers. In this circular motion a non-erring motion is given to the soul which returns and gathers the soul from the many which are outside it. It is first returned into itself and then, as it comes to be of one form, it is singly united with its unifying powers; in this way it is conducted to the beautiful and good beyond all things: the one and the same, without beginning and end.
> The soul moves spirally insofar as it has been illuminated with the divine knowledge in a manner appropriate to it: not intellectually and simply, but logically and discursively, according to its mixed and changing activities. Now the straight motion of the soul is not its entrance into itself (for this is a circular motion, as has been said); rather, in

WHY CONTEMPLATE?

this motion it proceeds away from those outside of it to those about it, just as it is led from many and various symbols to simple and unified contemplations.[8]

As with Nietzsche's parable, there is much of interest to say about this passage. We could talk about its sources in Platonism and Neoplatonism, about the differences between angelic and human motions and how they are leagued to modes of knowing. I shall not venture on any of those trails, though, and shall confine myself only to the movements that are described. There are just three of them: circular, spiral, and linear. The soul performs a circular motion when it passes from the external world to its own spiritual reality, and, on reflecting on itself, as we have seen time and again in earlier chapters, it curves upward to God. If the soul engages in discursive reasoning about God, as happens when one reads philosophy or theology, it enacts a spiral movement, since time is involved. One slowly winds upwards to the deity. Finally, if the soul looks to phenomena, reflects on them, and so rises above them to God, it traces out a straight line.

We know next to nothing about the actual circumstances of Dionysius the Areopagite, not his given name or his dates of birth and death. He hid himself from even the most exacting modern scholarly gaze very effectively indeed. Even if he was cloistered and relatively immune to the turmoil of his day, he could not have been entirely insulated from certain things. Bubonic plague ravaged what we take to be his land, and there was a Muslim conquest of Roman-occupied Syria with all the violence that such routs leave in their wake. He, too, might have been touched by disaster. Yet the inner movements he proposes

WHY CONTEMPLATE?

to himself and to his readers lead from experiences of being broken, deficient, or scattered to becoming one with the deity. Where Nietzsche diagnoses our situation, which is worse for us than it was for him, and which can at best fascinate us, Pseudo-Dionysius advocates the contemplation of the deity beyond even our most elevated notions of being. Let us see what is at issue in this distinction.

▶ ▷ ▶

We all know what it is to be fascinated by something or someone. Our first sense of being overtaken by fascination is likely to be curiosity, interest, even absorption, in a project, movie, game, or scene unfolding before us. We begin to understand fascination better, though, when we realize that the experience constrains us; it is as though we cannot release ourselves from looking at the iPhone, the laptop screen, or even from constantly brooding about something we dread or desire. When fascinated, we cannot think properly; our minds spin round and round. It's an attitude, Husserl would say, just as contemplation is, but the former is stultifying, and the latter is generative. The word comes to us from the Latin *fascinatio*, an act of bewitchment, and it enters English by way of French in the late sixteenth century. If we go deep enough into the origins of the word, we shall find that it bespeaks being enchanted, whether by a serpent or a witch. It was long believed that the eyes can send out rays that can have evil effects. In ancient Rome, victorious generals rewarded by the Senate with a Triumph through the city placed beneath their chariot a *fascinum*, an ivory phallus that was believed to deflect the rays of envious eyes that could cast a curse. Handsome

WHY CONTEMPLATE?

young men also wore a fascinum around their necks as an amulet; beautiful women would have the symbol on rings and would hang a charm around their baby's neck. Some cultures still believe in the "evil eye," but, even if one has no such belief, one knows, often all too well, what it is to be in the grip of something, whether real or imagined.

Language changes, and today the word "fascinate" has come to seem far more benign than it was several hundred years ago. We sometimes talk about being fascinated by a conversation, a novel, a TV show, when all that is meant is that we have become strongly interested in it. The elements of overwhelming intensity and danger have faded from the word's colloquial meaning. Yet the popular sense of the word and the concept behind it do not fully converge, even now. Our age is one of relentless enchantment with one thing or another in the negative sense of the word. The media has us transfixed by images of Hollywood stars, media celebrities, renowned or abominated politicians, and calamities that are brought to the many screens we have before us over the course of a day. "I could not put it down" is a common testament or lament. It is a lament when we realize, sometimes despite ourselves, that we have become addicted to something that enthralls us—social media, terrible car accidents seen while driving on the freeway, stories about violent events, even hurricanes on the weather channel—and that, after a while, our experience is only one of prolonged emptiness. The image is before us, it takes us in, and we cannot extract ourselves so easily from its pull. Bright as these images are, their deepest truth is that our experience these days is often of being unchained, going this way and that, without any direction, with a sense of heading only into the dark.[9]

WHY CONTEMPLATE?

This is a large part of what Nietzsche meant by "God is dead." Even if one goes to church, synagogue, mosque, or temple, even if one says prayers at home, the chances are that one does so in the wake of the death of God. For all intents and purposes, he has died in our daily lives, which go on, taking almost all our attention, regardless of what we tell ourselves we believe most deeply. He has died in our minds: our understanding does not see him luminously at the end of our desire to know. And he has died in our hearts: we seek ultimate satisfaction elsewhere, in family, work, travel, and pleasure. It is not exclusively a modern event, but it has come to characterize Western modernity. When people arrive at this realization, they will sometimes become drawn to contemplation, and, once they begin to practice it, in one mode or another, they start to see concretely how it differs from fascination.

Just as the word "fascination" has increased in use in recent times, the word "contemplation" has decreased over the same period while nonetheless expanding its semantic range. In colloquial speech, "contemplation" can mean no more than forethought, planning, or reflection; it can even cover some of the meanings associated today with "fascination." Yet when people are drawn to learn how to contemplate, they go past these newer linguistic resonances and seek the older strata of the word. They may not know it, but they pass from what Nietzsche has told us to what the Pseudo-Dionysius tells us. They might not follow Pseudo-Dionysius's strongly Platonic bent, or show any interest in the divine names or the God beyond being. After all, contemplation can be performed in many keys, including contemporary ones. Yet those same people are

WHY CONTEMPLATE?

likely to have acutely sensed the emptiness and disorientation that Nietzsche puts before us.

To get our bearings, let us recall Richard of St. Victor, whose *The Ark of Moses* we have considered, all too briefly, in chapters 2 and 3. Richard also knew about fascination, though his experience of it was vastly different to ours. He knew in particular that sin is endlessly fascinating, and that fascination has a great ability to tempt human beings. As a priest, he doubtless played a role in releasing the people he served outside Paris from thoughts and actions that paralyzed them, promising riches and giving only emptiness. His concern was not, like mine, to examine the phased counterparts of fascination and contemplation; it was, rather, to distinguish thinking, meditating, and contemplating. In *The Ark of Moses*, Richard defers to the late, great theologian at the Abbey, Hugh of St. Victor: "Contemplation is the penetrating and free view (*contuitus*) of the mind extended everywhere in perceiving things."[10] See how this conception of things differs from what we have seen of fascination? It stresses three things. Contemplation is penetrating; it is free; and it is extended everywhere. The Latin noun *contuitus* means "attentive view" or "gaze," but the translator is not wrong to call it a "free view," for both Hugh and Richard regard contemplation as an openness to what is beheld. One can set one's gaze anywhere at all, on the physical, intellectual, or divine.

First, contemplation is penetrating. When we engage in it, we find that we can go deeper into the object set before the mind than we can at other times. We pierce through its barriers and enter into hidden inner depths, and we return to normal life with more insight into what has come under

WHY CONTEMPLATE?

our gaze. Of course, this does not always happen, and it often helps to prepare for the time of contemplation. Thoughtful attention, including preliminary reading, with respect to what one wishes to behold can be invaluable. Second, contemplation is a freely adopted gaze. There is no sense of compulsion or constraint when reflecting on the object before one. Nor is there any obstacle that is encountered. With practice, distractions can be dealt with. One is free to ponder any profile of an object and to follow it wherever it prompts one to go. One is free to go up or down, as it were, from left to right or from right to left, and around and around in a circle. Yet if one moves in a circular manner, one's mind will be enriched and will not merely spin. One is never held against one's will by the object of reflection, but sometimes a sense of wonder and delight will stretch the act longer than one would ever have thought likely. And, third, contemplation is extended everywhere. There are no limits encountered; the act opens onto infinite horizons that are always fresh. When one has been fascinated, one returns to normal life depleted and dry, and when one has contemplated, the return comes with a sense of refreshment and increased understanding.

People who have experienced even a little of what Nietzsche's madman proclaims know well enough to take care of themselves. And one does not need to plumb the depths of nihilism to realize that modern life, with its culture of fascination, cannot be pursued without some respite from it. Spiritual exercises can help now, as they once helped Epicureans, Stoics, and Platonists in ancient Greece. Many people regain a fuller, richer sense of life by practicing *smṛti*. Those drawn to spending time in the country, viewing art or reading poetry, can cultivate aesthetic

WHY CONTEMPLATE?

contemplation. And those with philosophical training can read deeply in Husserl or Wittgenstein and attempt a more contemplative attitude to the big questions of being, knowing, and acting. Whatever else we do, those of us in the Abrahamic faiths will wish to cultivate mental prayer. Christians, in particular, will look to lectio divina. The important thing is to ensure that the exercise is undertaken with all due concentration and to do it each day and not yield when periods of flatness and spiritual dryness come, as they surely will. The movements of the soul are at least as essential to life as the motions of the body.

Notes

1. First Thoughts About Contemplation

1. Needless to say, perhaps, there have been attempts to recover the practice: the Centering Prayer project, for instance, which has been taken up by Protestants as well as Catholics. To some extent, the same can be said of the Taizé community in France.
2. The Jesus Prayer runs as follows: "Lord Jesus Christ, Son of the living God, have mercy on me, a sinner."
3. See Roberto Juarroz, *Fragments verticaux*, traduit de l'espagnol par Silvia Baron Supervielle (Paris: José Corti, 1994), § 174.
4. See Aristotle, *Metaphysics*, ed. Hugh Tredennick (Cambridge, Mass.: Harvard University Press, 1933), 982b; and *Nicomachean Ethics*, ed. H. Rackham (Cambridge, Mass.: Harvard University Press, 1934), book 10.
5. Pseudo-Dionysius the Areopagite, *The Mystical Theology*, in *The Divine Names and Mystical Theology*, trans. and intro. by John D. Johns (Milwaukee: Marquette University Press, 1980) chapter 1.
6. Pseudo-Dionysius, *Mystical Theology*, chapter 1.
7. Philo, *On the Unchangeableness of God*, trans. F. H. Colson and G. H. Whitaker (Cambridge, Mass.: Harvard University Press, 1930), 37:181–82.
8. Origen, *Homilies on Numbers*, ed. Christopher A. Hall, trans. Thomas P. Scheck (Westmont, Ill.: Intervarsity, 2009),15:1.

1. FIRST THOUGHTS ABOUT CONTEMPLATION

9. See Jean-Pierre de Caussade, *The Sacrament of the Present Moment*, intro. Richard M. Forster, trans. Kitty Muggeridge (New York: Harper and Row, 1982). Whether de Caussade is the author of the text has been strongly contested in recent times. See also St. Francis de Sales, *Treatise on the Love of God* (Radford, Va.: Wilder, 2022), books 8 and 9.

2. Questions of Practice and Cognition

1. Richard of St. Victor, *The Ark of Moses*, trans. Ineke Van't Spijker and Hugh Feiss, in *Spiritual Formation and Mystical Symbolism*, ed. Grover A. Zinn, Dale M. Coulter, and Franz van Liere (Turnhout, Belgium: Brepols, 2022), 10:1.3. For further detail on Richard, see my book *Lands of Likeness: For a Poetics of Contemplation* (Chicago: University of Chicago Press, 2023).
2. Richard of St. Victor, *Ark of Moses*, 10:1.5. It is important to distinguish the movements of the soul in contemplative prayer from the emotions that are also sometimes called "movements of the soul" in moral theology.
3. Edmund Husserl, *Ideas for a Pure Phenomenology and Phenomenological Philosophy, 1: General Introduction to Pure Phenomenology*, trans. Daniel O. Dahlstrom (Indianapolis: Hackett, 2014), § 27.
4. Edmund Husserl, *The Crisis of European Sciences and Transcendental Phenomenology: An Introduction to Phenomenological Philosophy*, trans. David Carr (Evanston: Northwestern University Press 1970), 52.
5. See Kevin Hart, *Kingdoms of God* (Bloomington: Indiana University Press, 2014).
6. Rolland to Freud, December 5, 1927, quoted in William Parsons, *The Enigma of the Oceanic Feeling: Revisioning the Psychoanalytic Theory of Mysticism* (Oxford: Oxford University Press, 1999), 36.
7. Thomas Aquinas, *Summa theologiae*, gen. ed. Thomas Gilby, 60 vols. (London: Eyre and Spottiswoode, 1964–1980), 1a q. 4 art. 2.
8. Aquinas, *Summa theologiæ*, 1a q. 8 art. 1.
9. Teresa of Ávila, *Life*, trans. E. Allison Peers (New York: Doubleday, 1960). It is worth noting that Bernard McGinn titles his magisterial seven-volume history of mysticism *The Presence of God* (1991–2021).

10. De Caussade, *The Sacrament of the Present Moment*, trans. Kitty Muggeridge (New York: HarperOne, 1989), 5.
11. Bernard of Clairvaux, *Sermons on the Song of Songs*, trans. Kilian Walsh, 4 vols. (Collegeville, Minn.: Liturgical, 1971), 74.2.5.

3. Ways of Contemplating

1. The original Creed of 381 has the Holy Spirit proceeding from the Father only. In 1054 the Catholic Church added the *filioque* clause "and the Son," thereby changing the Creed and precipitating a division between the Roman Catholics and the Orthodox.
2. Aquinas, *Summa theologiæ*, gen. ed. Thomas Gilby (London: Eyre and Spottiswoode, 1964–1980), 1a q. 1 art. 4 resp.
3. Aquinas, *Summa theologiæ*, 1a q. 1 art. 1 resp.
4. Aquinas, *Summa theologiæ*, 1a q. 1 art. 2 resp.
5. See Cicero, *Tusculan Disputations*, ed. John Edward King, Loeb Classical Library, rev. ed. (Cambridge, Mass.: Harvard University Press, 1927).
6. Only fragments of *Hortensius* have come down to us.
7. See Bernadette Roberts, *The Experience of No-Self: A Contemplative Journey*, 2nd ed. (Albany: State University of New York Press, 1993).
8. It is important to stress that objections to hesychasm mostly constellate in the Latin rite of the Catholic Church. To be sure, it is the largest rite of the Church, but there are six other rites, including whole families of rites, such as those of the Eastern Catholics.
9. Aquinas, *Commentary on the Gospel of John*, 3 vols., trans. Fabian Larcher and James A. Weisheipl, intro. and notes by Daniel Keating and Matthew Levering (Washington, D.C.: Catholic University of America Press, 2010), vol. 1, § 211.
10. See Aristotle, *Categories*, trans. Harold Percy Cooke (Cambridge, Mass.: Harvard University Press, 1938), 1b25–2a4.
11. Aquinas, *Summa theologiæ*, 1a q. 3 art. 1 A.D. 1.
12. See Johannes Zachhuber, "Transcendence and Immanence," in *The Edinburgh Critical History of Nineteenth-Century Christian Theology*, ed. Daniel Whistler (Edinburgh: Edinburgh University Press, 2017), 164–81.

3. WAYS OF CONTEMPLATING

13. See, above all, Pierre Hadot, *Philosophy as a Way of Life* (Oxford: Wiley-Blackwell, 1995). See also Michel Foucault, *The History of Sexuality*, vol. 3: *The Care of the Self* (New York: Vintage, 1988).
14. See Hadot, *Don't Forget to Live: Goethe and the Tradition of Spiritual Exercises*, trans. Michael Chase (Chicago: University of Chicago Press, 2023).
15. See Edmund Husserl, *On the Phenomenology of the Consciousness of Internal Time (1893–1917)*, ed. John Barnett Brough (Dordrecht: Springer, 1991), 1, §§ 10, 12, 29, and passim.
16. On this topic, see Nicole Kelley, "Philosophy as Training for Death: Reading the Ancient Christian Martyr Acts as Spiritual Exercises," *Church History* 75, no. 4 (2006), 723–47.
17. Jean Pierre De Caussade, *The Sacrament of the Present Moment*, trans. Kitty Muggeridge (New York: HarperOne, 1989), 46.
18. Dante, *Paradiso*, trans. Philip H. Wickstead and Herman Oelsner (London: J. M. Dent and Sons, 1919), 3:85.
19. De Caussade, *Sacrament of the Present Moment*, 79.
20. Richard of St. Victor, *On the Ark of Moses*, ed. Grover A. Zinn, Dale M. Coulter and Frans van Liere, intro. Dale M. Coulter, and trans. Ineke Van't Spijker and Hugh Feiss, (Turnhout, Belgium: Brepols, 2022), 1.3. It should be noted that Richard's *The Book of the Patriarchs* consider the preparations for contemplation.
21. The idea of a beings as more or less real is also affirmed in British idealism. In his *Appearance and Reality* ([1893] 1897), F. H. Bradley, for example, contends that the Absolute is perfect reality whereas everything else in the universe has lesser or greater degrees of reality.
22. Aquinas, *Commentary*, vol. 1, § 18.
23. See Aquinas, *Scriptum super Sententiis* (Rochester, N.Y.: Aquinas Institute, forthcoming), 3 Sent. d. 36 q. 1 a. 3 a 5.
24. Gregory is presumably alluding to John 8:25 as rendered in the Vulgate: *Dicebant ergo ei tu quis es dixit eis Iesus principium quia et loquor vobis.* Reference to Gregory is constant in the treatise on action and contemplation in the *Summa theologiæ*. In the *Scriptum super sententiis*, Aquinas makes the same point with reference to Aristotle in *Nicomachean Ethics*, 10. See 3 Sent. d. 35 a. 2 qu. 3. See also *Summa theologiæ*, 1a q. 3 art. 5, resp.

4. WHAT TO CONTEMPLATE

25. See Aquinas, *Summa theologiæ*, 1a q. 2 art. 3 resp.; and *Summa Contra Gentiles*, trans. Anton Charles Pegis (South Bend, Ind.: Notre Dame University Press, 1975), 1.13.
26. See Hugh of St. Victor, Sermon 72, *Patrologia Latina*, ed. Jacques-Paul Migne (Paris: Garnier, 1881–1865), 177, col. 1131.
27. Aquinas, *Summa theologiæ*, 2a2æ q. 180 art. 4 ad 3. Aquinas often uses *consideratio* or one of its forms beginning with the *Scriptum super Sententiis* and especially in the second part of the *Summa theologiæ*.
28. See Aquinas, 3 Sent. d. 35 q.1 2 qu. 3, resp.; and Aristotle, *Nicomachean Ethics*, trans. H. Rackham (Cambridge, Mass.: Harvard University Press, 1934), 9.8. Aristotle is himself following Greek emphasis on contemplation as a way of life.
29. Aquinas, *Summa theologiæ*, 2a2æ q. 175 art. 3 resp.

4. What to Contemplate

1. Iamblichus, *On the Pythagorean Way of Life*, ed. John M. Dillon and Jackson Hershbell (Atlanta, Ga.: Society of Biblical Literature, 1991), chapter 12.
2. Plato, *Republic*, books 6–10, trans. Paul Shorey (Cambridge, Mass.: Harvard University Press, 1935), 517d-e.
3. Plato, *Phaedrus*, 247 d-e, in *Euthyphro, Apology Crito, Phaedo, Phaedrus*, trans. Harold North Fowler, intro. W. R. M. Lamb, Loeb Classical Library (Cambridge, Mass.: Harvard University Press, 1914).
4. Justin Martyr, *Dialogue with Trypho*, 8, and *The Second Apology*, 2.13, in *The First Apology, The Second Apology, Dialogue with Trypho, Exhortation to the Greeks, Discourse to the Greeks, The Monarchy or the Rule of God*, trans. Thomas B. Falls, the Fathers of the Church (Washington, D.C.: Catholic University of America Press, 2010).
5. Plato, *Timaeus*, 27d 5f, in *Timaeus, Critias, Cleitophon, Menixenus, Epistles*, trans. R. G. Bury, Loeb Classical Library (Cambridge, Mass.: Harvard University Press, 1929).
6. Aristotle, *Nicomachean Ethics*, trans. H. Rackham, Loeb Classical Library (Cambridge, Mass.: Harvard University Press, 1926), 10.8, 1178b 7–32.
7. Plotinus, *Ennead 1*, trans. A. H. Armstrong, Loeb Classical Library (Cambridge, Mass. Harvard University Press, 1966), 1.6.9.

4. WHAT TO CONTEMPLATE

8. Plotinus, *Ennead 3*, trans. A. H. Armstrong, Loeb Classical Library (Cambridge, Mass.: Harvard University Press, 1967), 3.8.4.
9. Augustine, "On True Religion," trans. Edmund Hill, 39.72, in *On Christian Belief*, gen. intro. and other intros. by Michael Fiedrowicz, ed. Boniface Ramsey, *The Works of Saint Augsutine*, vol. 8, sec. 1 (Hyde Park, N.Y.: New City, 2005).
10. Basil of Caesarea, "On the Hexæmeron," in *Exegetic Homilies*, trans. Agnes Clare Way, The Fathers of the Church (Washington, D.C.: Catholic University of America Press, 1963), homily 6.1.
11. Immanuel Kant, *The Critique of Judgement*, trans. James Creed Meredith (Oxford: Clarendon Press, 1952), § 5. Also see § 12.
12. See C. S. Lewis, *Perelandra* (New York: Scribner, [1943] 2003).
13. Søren Kierkegaard, *The Concept of Irony with Continual Reference to Socrates, Notes of Schelling's Berlin Lectures*, ed. and trans. Howard V. Hong and Edna H. Hong, *Kierkegaard's Writings*, vol. 2 (Princeton, N.J.: Princeton University Press, 1989), 272. Aurora's husband was Tithonus, who was granted immortality but not youth and therefore wasted almost entirely away. Kierkegaard later evokes what he calls K. W. F. Solger's "contemplative irony," which reflects on the nothingness of everything, *The Concept of Irony with Constant Reference to Socrates*, ed. and trans. Howard V. Hong and Edna H. Hong (Princeton, N.J.: Princeton University Press, 1989), 309.
14. Arthur Schopenhauer, *The World as Will and Representation*, ed. Christopher Janaway, ed. and trans. Judith Norman and Alistair Welchman (Cambridge: Cambridge University Press, 2010), 201.
15. Schopenhauer, *World as Will and Representation*, 1:234.
16. For more information, see Stephen Cross, *Schopenhauer's Encounter with Indian Thought: "Representation and Will" and their Indian Parallels* (Honolulu: University of Hawai'i Press, 2013).
17. Schopenhauer, *World as Will and Representation*, 1:8.
18. Ludwig Wittgenstein, *Philosophical Investigations*, 2nd ed., trans. G. E. M. Anscombe (Oxford: Basil Blackwell, 1958), § 133d.
19. Wittgenstein, *Philosophical Investigations*, § 309.
20. Wittgenstein, *Culture and Value*, 2nd ed., ed. Georg Henrik von Wright in collaboration with Heikki Nyman, trans. Peter Winch (Oxford: Basil Blackwell, 1980), 5e.

21. Wittgenstein, *Zettel*, ed. G. E. M. Anscombe and G. H. von Wright, trans. G. E. M. Anscombe (Oxford: Basil Blackwell, 1967), § 447.
22. See D. Z. Phillips, *Philosophy's Cool Place* (Ithaca, N.Y.: Cornell University Press, 1989); and *Religion and the Hermeneutics of Contemplation* (Cambridge: Cambridge University Press, 2001).
23. See Martin Heidegger, "Science and Reflection," in *The Question Concerning Technology and Other Essays*, intro. and trans. William Lovitt (New York: Harper and Row, 1977), 155–82. See also his *Bremen and Freiburg Lectures: Insight Into That Which Is and Basic Principles of Thinking*, trans. Andrew J. Mitchell (Bloomington: Indiana University Press, 2012), 99.
24. For a rather different understanding of how poetry can be read contemplatively, see my *Lands of Likeness: For a Poetics of Contemplation* (Chicago: University of Chicago Press, 2023).

5. Why Contemplate?

1. See Ulrich L. Lehner, *Monastic Prisons and Torture Chambers: Crime and Punishment in Monasteries, 1600–1800* (Eugene, Or.: Cascade, 2013).
2. Margaret Porette, *The Mirror of Simple Souls*, trans. Edmund Colledge (Notre Dame, Ind.: University of Notre Dame Press, 1999), 66.
3. On the differences between lay brothers and choir monks, see James France, *Separate but Equal: Cistercian Lay Brothers, 1120–1350* (Collegeville, Mich.: Liturgical Press, 2012).
4. See Augustine, *The Work of Monks* in *Treatises on Various Subjects*, ed. Roy J. Deferrari, trans. Mary Sarah Muldowney (Washington, D.C.: Catholic University of America Press, 2002); and *The Rule of St. Benedict in English*, ed. Timothy Fry, foreword by Thomas Moore (Collegeville, Mich.: Liturgical Press, 1981).
5. On the relation of leisure and contemplation, see Joseph Pieper, *Happiness and Contemplation*, intro. Ralph McInerney (South Bend, Ind.: St. Augustine's, 1998); and *Leisure: The Basis of Culture*, foreword by James V. Schall (San Francisco, Calif.: Ignatius, 2009).
6. Aristotle, *Nicomachean Ethics*, trans. H. Rackham (Cambridge, Mass. Harvard University Press, 1934), book 10.

5. WHY CONTEMPLATE?

7. Friedrich Nietzsche, *The Gay Science: With a Prelude in Rhymes and an Appendix of Songs*, trans. Walter Kaufmann (New York: Vintage, 1974), §125.
8. Pseudo-Dionysius the Areopagite, *The Divine Names*, 4.9, in *The Divine Names and Mystical Theology*, trans. and intro. John D. Jones (Milwaukee, Wis.: Marquette University Press, 1980).
9. For further discussion of the image, see my *Maurice Blanchot on Poetry and Narrative: Ethics of the Image* (London: Bloomsbury, 2023), chapter 9.
10. Richard of St. Victor, *On the Ark of Moses*, in *Spiritual Formation and Mystical Symbolism*, intro. Dale M. Coulter, trans. Ineke Van't Spijker and Hugh Feiss (Turnhout, Belgium: Brepols, 2022), 260.

Further Reading

Badri, Malik. *Contemplation: An Islamic Psychospiritual Study*. Introduced by Jeremy Henzell-Thomas. Translated by Abdul-Wahid Lu'lu'a. Herndon, Va.: International Institute of Islamic Thought, 2000.

Feiner, Jonathan. *Mindfulness: A Jewish Approach*. Los Angeles: Mosaica, 2021.

Flood, Gavin. *The Truth Within: A History of Inwardness in Christianity, Hinduism, and Buddhism*. Oxford: Oxford University Press, 2013.

Hart, Kevin. *Lands of Likeness: For a Poetics of Contemplation*. Chicago: University of Chicago Press, 2023.

Hadot, Pierre. *Philosophy as a Way of Life: Spiritual Exercises from Socrates to Foucault*. Edited and introduced by Arnold I. Davidson. Translated by Michael Chase. Oxford: Basil Blackwell, 1995.

Kabot-Zinn, Jon. *Mindfulness for Beginners: Reclaiming the Present Moment and Your Life*. Louisville, Colo.: Sounds True, 2016.

Keating, Thomas. *Intimacy with God: An Introduction to Centering Prayer*. New York: Crossroads, [1994] 2019.

Komjathy, Louis, ed. *Contemplative Literature: A Comparative Sourcebook on Meditation and Contemplative Prayer*. Albany: State University of New York Press, 2015.

Merton, Thomas. *What Is Contemplation?* Springfield, Il.: Templegate, 1981.

Shaw, Sarah. *Introduction to Buddhist Meditation*. London: Routledge, 2009.

Index

Abandonment, 22, 66, 78–79
Allegory, 20–21
Angela of Foligno (St.), 19
Aquinas, Thomas (St.), 16, 52–53, 59–62, 67, 69, 79, 83–87, 92, 98, 115–16
Aristotle, 8–10, 16, 65, 68, 92–94, 96, 110, 122
Ascent, 79–81, 107
Augustine (St.), 16, 56, 65, 88, 97, 119
Aurelius, Marcus, 71–72

Bacon, Francis, 23
Basil of Caesarea (St.), 97
Benedict (St.), 40, 119
Bernard of Clairvaux (St.), 12, 54–57, 75, 84
Buddha, 4
Buddhism, 3–6, 8, 11, 49, 66, 73–75, 89, 105, 117, 122, 132

Caussade, Jean-Pierre de, 21–22, 54, 76–79
Chiyo-ni, 105
Cicero, 64–65
Consideration, 12–13, 61, 75, 84, 87. *See also* Meditation
Contemplation, 40, 45, 46, 62; aesthetic, 9, 29, 47, 100–1, 103–4, 106, 111, 120, 122, 132; natural, 9, 29, 94, 97; passive, 11, 36, 49, 54; phenomenological, 111, 114; vocations, 29, 53, 84, 87, 115–16, 117–18

Dante, 78

Epictetus, 70
Epicurus, 70
Experience, 23–26, 53–57, 59, 63, 66, 68–69, 86, 98

INDEX

Fascination, 122, 126, 128–32
Fénelon, François, 77
Freud, Sigmund, 25, 52

Galilei, Galileo, 23
God: Trinity, 16–17, 22, 60, 68, 82, 90; union with, 5, 14, 22, 54, 59, 63, 66
Goethe, J. W. von, 73–74
Gregory of Nyssa (St.), 75
Gregory the Great (St.), 85–86
Guyon, Jeanne, 19, 66, 77, 118

Hall, G. Stanley, 25
Hegel, G. W. F., 23, 51
Heidegger, Martin, 64, 113–14
Hesychasm, 6, 66–68, 77, 109, 120, 137 n. 8.
Hildegard of Bingen (St.), 62–63
Hinduism, 3, 7, 52, 57, 66, 89, 104
Homer, 20
Horace, 74
Hugh of St. Cher, 115
Hugh of St. Victor, 38, 44, 79, 87, 131
Husserl, Edmund, 9, 46–48, 106, 109–14, 128

Iamblichus, 90
Image, 11–12, 14, 31, 80–82, 129; of God, 34; of the Father, 4, 91
Intuition, 13, 14–15, 29, 53, 87, 98, 102, 107, 110, 115
Islam, 3, 7–8, 28, 56, 127

James, William, 25
John of the Cross (St.), 66, 77, 119
Juarroz, Roberto, 9

Julian of Norwich, 62
Justin Martyr, 92

Kant, Immanuel, 23, 64, 69–70, 98–100, 102–6, 110, 112

Lectio divina, 40–46, 49, 133
Locke, John, 23, 64
Lombard, Peter, 84, 86
Love, 6, 14, 18–19, 22, 26, 34, 40–41, 44, 46, 49, 56–57, 61, 63–64, 76, 78–79, 83, 87–88, 100, 118; and disinterest, 101; self-love, 66
Loyola, Ignatius (St.), 75, 77
Lucretius, 70

McKeon, Richard, 109
Meditation, 10–14, 31–38, 41–44, 48, 73, 75, 122. *See also* Consideration
Methley, Richard, 19
Mindfulness, 8
Modernity, 21, 24, 90, 124, 130
Modus sine modo, 56
Molinos, Miguel de, 77
Muhammed, 28
Mystical theology, 15–18, 20, 26
Mysticism, 15, 19, 22–23, 25, 53, 59, 66, 89

Needler, Henry, 98
Newton, John, 23
Nietzsche, Friedrich, 123–28, 130–32
Nirvana, 5

Origen, 21–22
Otto, Rudolph, 25

INDEX

Palamas, Gregory (St.), 67
Paul (St.), 16, 20, 51, 55, 88, 91, 119
Perec, Georges, 101
Phillips, D. Z., 109
Philo Judaeus, 21–22, 27
Philosophy, 7, 23, 63–65, 94, 107–8; Christianity as true philosophy, 92; as contemplative, 9, 109–10; and religion, 8, 68; and science, 93
Plato, 64–65, 70–71, 75, 80–81, 90–93, 95, 97, 103, 105, 110, 127, 130, 132
Plotinus, 94–96
Ponge, Francis, 101
Porette, Margaret, 19, 117–18
Porphyry, 95
Prayer, 5–6, 14, 22, 26, 29, 34, 37, 41, 43, 46, 50–51, 62, 66–68, 76, 97, 115, 117, 119–21
Presence, 24, 32, 35, 37, 44, 50–57, 62, 82
Proclus, 16, 20
Pseudo-Dionysius, 16–18, 20, 22, 77, 88, 126–28, 130
Pythagoras, 90

Quietism, 77, 89, 100; philosophical, 107

Raphael, 94
Reduction, 112
Rhees, Rush, 109
Richard of St. Victor, 38–41, 44, 79–83, 86–87, 89–90, 97, 104, 131

Roberts, Bernadette, 66, 89
Rolland, Romain, 51
Roussel, Raymond, 101

Sales, François de (St.), 21, 77–79
Saussure, H. B. de, 99
Schleiermacher, Friedrich, 23–24
Schopenhauer, Arthur, 102–6, 111–12
Simplicius, 94
Spiritual exercises, 5, 7, 63, 70–75, 120–22, 132

Templum, 26–27
Teresa of Ávila (St.), 26, 53–54, 119
Theagenes of Rhegium, 20
Theology, 9, 61, 65, 84; apophatic, 19; cataphatic, 18–19. *See also* Mystical theology
Theoroi, 27, 90
Thinking, 38, 40–43, 45, 49, 79, 112, 131
Transcendence, 65, 69–70
Transcendentals, 68–69
Tout dire, 101, 110

Underhill, Evelyn, 25

Virtue, 9, 83, 92, 94–96, 107, 118
Vodolazkin, Eugene, 120
Von Hügel, Friedrich, 25

Winch, Peter, 109
Wittgenstein, Ludwig, 9, 106–9, 133
Wunt, William, 25

147